The Other Side
of Grief

The Other Side of Grief

ELIZABETH FITCH

Oakwood Farm Press, LLC

Cover photograph and design by Matthew McCormick.
Book design by Jenny Yoshida Park, Evidence of the Hand.

To my husband
who loved me
through the storm
and out again

Contents

Grief Like A Storm

The rain to the wind said,
"You push and I'll pelt."
They so smote the garden bed
That the flowers actually knelt
And lay lodged—though not dead.
I know how the flowers felt.

Robert Frost[1]

Grief hits like a storm. It blindsides you. It changes life as you knew it.

It happened to me when I lost my father. In the pain and confusion, I started writing letters to him. I wrote most of them on days when I wanted to talk to him so badly that it hurt. I wrote during some of the blackest moments of my life. It let me give grief the space it needs.

The letters are raw and rough, and one piece doesn't fit neatly with the next, but that's how grief is. Nothing about it fits neatly. Nothing about it makes sense at the time. You can't anticipate it or outline it or explain it. Not even to the person closest to you. Not even to yourself.

I know that my loss isn't exactly the same as your loss. Losing your father isn't the same as losing your child or your marriage or your health or your job. It isn't the same as the grief of never having known a father's love or a mother's or a child's. But grief is grief, and grieving people understand each other.

One broken heart hears another.

It helped me along the way to listen to people who had been there before me. It helped me to hear some of the things they went through. Sometimes it kept me from adding the pain of wondering if I was going crazy to the pain of losing my father.

I hope as you read this book you will hear one thing loud and clear: you are not alone. C. S. Lewis once said that friendship is born when one person says to another, "What? You, too? I thought I was the only one."[2] You're not the only one, and I'm not, either.

I hope that my words will give you the courage to give grief the space it needs. I hope that they will give you permission to feel the pain. And, most of all, I hope that they will point you toward the glimmers of hope downstream.

If you grieve well, joy does come in the morning. Gradually, you find that God is with you in the dark. Gradually, He fills the empty space. Gradually, life wins. That's because grief is a love word. It is a scary word and a dark word and a painful word, but it is also a love word.

The letters to my father were birthed in scary and dark and painful times. They weren't written for an audience, so I never gave any thought to providing the kind of context that would make a reader comfortable. I want you to be comfortable and undistracted by questions, so here is some background information that may help.

My father's name is Carlton Byrd. He lived all his life on the Eastern Shore of Virginia, near the Chesapeake Bay. He left the Eastern Shore for college and then he left to fight a war. Other than that, I think he only left to please somebody or to help somebody. The Eastern Shore was his place. It was in his blood.

He was a farmer, like his father before him. He started a small farming business in the early 1950s, and a few decades later he was growing and packing a million boxes of tomatoes a year. People who know the tomato business say that he was the best tomato farmer on the east coast—maybe the best in the whole country.

He worked hard. In the summer months, he worked 15-hour days. It was the kind of business that could make a lot of money one year and then lose it all the next year. He liked that. It kept him young.

Home was ten minutes away from the business. It was his other world. We lived on a creek. (On the Eastern Shore, we call rivers "creeks.") We lived in a house that he and Mom built when I was a toddler. There were three of us girls. He thought we hung the moon, and he showed it gently and extravagantly. His home life was calm and ordered and filled with women. His business life was frenzied and messy and filled mostly with men. He moved between the two worlds easily, and he was very careful not to let them meet.

No matter how hard things got, he never quit. Toward the end of his life, some very hard things happened. A stroke stole his ability to read and write. The business went into bankruptcy (and came out the other end, mostly because he wouldn't take no for an answer). He never gave up.

On his last day, which was Easter of 2006, he drove through his fields looking at the baby tomato plants, and then he came home and sat down on his porch by the creek and had a heart attack. Mom found him, and nothing has been quite the same since. He is buried in a far corner of the yard, and now Mom is, too.

The summer after he died, we sold the business. We sold everything except the land. We even sold the crop in the fields, and it turned out to be the best crop in fifty years. I worked for the next few years to finalize the sale and wade through a few lawsuits, but I was just mopping up. The main show ended when he died.

I used to talk with him by phone almost every day. I lived with my husband and children in the city, about four hours away from him and the creek and the business, and we visited back and forth. The children used to bask in his love. I think they still do, even though he has been gone for nine years now. These are the words that I spoke at his funeral:

My father was a great tomato farmer, but that wasn't what he did best. He was best at something much bigger. He was best at fathering, and his fathering shaped my whole world.

When I was little, the best moment of my day was when he came home from work. I would wait by the door with my collection of slippers and anything else that I thought he might like. When he put me to bed, he would brush my hair—a hundred strokes, he would say, until it shone. And then he would say good night and start to leave, and I would beg him to lie down, just for a few minutes, because I knew that in a few minutes he would be sound asleep beside me. Then I would bask in safety.

Nothing I did could make him love me more, and nothing I did could make him love me less. At eleven, I wrecked his best car. I was crying upstairs when he got home. He came and sat beside me. I said, "I'm so sorry. Your car is ruined." He said it was all right. I said, "But how much do you think it will cost to fix?"

"Fifty dollars," he said. "Just fifty dollars."

I was never afraid when he was with me. I remember how he used to take me into the surf in Ocean City. We would stand side-by-side, holding hands, and the waves that had seemed so scary when I was alone were just exciting and fun when my hand was in his. It wasn't until years later that I realized that I was a better swimmer than he was.

He was unflappable. In my early twenties, when I took him out to breakfast to tell him that I was going to marry my boyfriend and live on an island off the coast of Nova Scotia collecting seaweed for a living, he just sat calmly eating his eggs. Not even my wildest plans could shake his confidence in me, but that must have been a very long breakfast.

He taught me that I was his delight and that I was safe in his love. When I grew up and learned that my Father in heaven finds me delightful and that I am safe in His love, it was easy to believe. Papa had mirrored it every day of my life.

Today, my two fathers are together. I'm reminded of a comment made years ago by Dwight L. Moody: "One day you will open the newspaper and read that D. L. Moody of Chicago, Illinois, has died. Don't you believe *a word of it. I shall be more alive then than I am now."*[3] *So Papa is more alive now than he has ever been. For us I grieve, but for him I rejoice. For all we know, he just may be growing the best tomatoes ever—without worrying about the weather.*

I said these things before my heart realized that he was gone.

The Letters

Summer 2006

*Trusting even when it appears you
have been forsaken, praying when it
seems your words are simply entering a
vast expanse where no one hears and
no voice answers; believing that God's
love is complete and that He is aware
of your circumstances, even when your
world seems to grind on as if setting its
own direction ... this is genuine faith.*

George MacDonald[4]

Dear Papa,

Everything is different now. Two nights ago, in the middle of the night, everything changed.

I have a lot of middle-of-the-night time now. I've sort of forgotten how to sleep since you left. For a week or so, I slept pretty well, but that was only because of the pills.

I guess that was one difference between you and me—you loved pills, and I hated them. Or maybe that's not fair. Maybe you were just willing to take a whole pharmacy-full of pills every morning because you loved life so much.

Anyway, that's all behind you now. Nothing in you is broken any more. Nothing hurts. Now you could button buttons and get your arm in the sleeve on the first try. But I guess you don't have to bother now, do you?

What's it like waking up to a fresh new day, bursting with energy? Or do you wake up? Maybe there aren't any nights in heaven. If there are, though, I bet they're full of that deep sleep that leaves you breathless to start a new day.

I know your nights here were hard toward the end. You'd lie awake for hours, wandering back through the days and years, and then you'd catch up on your sleep during the day in your chair. On my last few visits, you fell asleep every time the family conversation could go on comfortably without you. The more you did that, the more I thought you'd be leaving for good soon. Maybe you thought so, too.

Anyway, everything feels different for me now because, in the deep of the night a few nights ago, joy came back. It came out of the blue. I woke up in the dark like I always do, thinking about you being gone like I always do, and then, all of a sudden, it was okay. I was glad that you were gone—glad that all the trying is over and that you'll never dread nursing homes again and that your whole world is bathed and shimmering with love like my garden the morning after a good rain.

And then came the very best part. I remembered that you're not gone forever. How did I miss for two whole months the joy of remembering that someday I'll be with you again? We'll talk again. We'll laugh again. I'll see your smile again, and the twinkle in your eye.

Until I get there, enjoy every single bit of heaven,

and I'll try to do the same thing here. We'll have some tales to tell each other, won't we, next time I hear, "Hi, my darling"?

Never again will they hunger; never again will they thirst.... God will wipe every tear from their eyes. There will be no more death or mourning or crying or pain.

Revelation 7:16-17; 21:4

Dear Papa,

You would like today. It's hot, and all the hundreds of acres of tomatoes that you planted are growing fast, making up for lost time. Even you wouldn't need a jacket today—just whatever cap took your fancy.

Today I'm remembering you without any tears. I remember how your face always lit up when I walked into the room. I remember how you ate crispy bacon with your pinkie in the air, as if you were at a tea party instead of a greasy diner. I remember how you always thought ahead of me when I came home, so that whatever I needed was taken care of, usually before I woke up in the morning. You always remembered me, and I guess that's why now, when you're gone, I always remember you.

If you were still here, we would be at your house today, sipping coffee and talking about your business. For as long as I can remember, whenever you talked about your office, you always said "my place." It was your refuge for decades, but things changed during your last few years. I could tell that you knew it really wasn't your place any more. Most of your people didn't stick by you when you got older. You must have hated that, but you never gave up.

26

I admire the way you weren't afraid in your world. You took risks, and you made things happen. I'm not nearly as brave as you were. I know that now, because I spend my days trying to run your business, scrambling to fill your shoes. (By the way, I've found out that it isn't *my* place, either.)

I miss you today. I miss you a whole lot. But I'm glad, too. I'm glad you don't need help getting dressed today. I'm glad your ears don't ring any more. I'm glad you don't walk sideways and stooped over anymore, and I'm glad I don't have to tell you anymore how debonair a cane looks. Neither of us ever believed that anyway.

I wonder what wonders fill your days now.

I love you this fine morning, and, at least for this one moment, loving you isn't breaking my heart.

Godspeed, my Papa. Happy Father's Day.

Do not let your hearts be troubled....
My Father's house has many rooms; ... I
am going there to prepare a place for you.

John 14:1-2

Dear Papa,

It's raining hard—thirteen inches already in some places. If you were still farming, you would make believe the rain didn't matter. You would say that tomato plants have nine lives, just like cats.

Yesterday, I ran in the rain for a long time. I ran past yards that had purple martin birdhouses, and I thought of you. I don't have many regrets, but I regret not getting you a purple martin house. I knew you always wanted one, and I never got around to buying you one. It would have brought you joy, but I kept forgetting. You never forgot the things that brought me joy.

At least I gave you the little ordinary bird feeders. Remember how we would wonder together why all the finches liked the feeders at my house better than the ones at your house? Well, a few weeks ago, I found all your feeders packed away in a box in a corner of the shed at your house, and I brought them back home with me and hung them outside my office window. Now you have plenty of finches. Maybe someday I'll get a purple martin house and watch them for you, too.

I found your little hibachi grill, too. It was just sitting there in the shed gathering dust. One glance at that grill, and I was a kid again watching you in your rocking chair in front of the fireplace cooking our steaks. I thought everybody charcoaled steaks in the living room, but it turns out it was only you.

It turns out that a lot of things were only you, and I never knew it until you left. Only you called me every day just to hear my voice. The boys told me that I should call them instead now. I do sometimes, but I get voicemail when they're in class, and then I miss you even more.

From now on, I think I'll just write you letters and try to remember to be happy that you're free. That's hard for me today. I'm glad it's not hard for you. I'm glad you live in an ocean of joy.

*Turn to me and be gracious to me, for
I am lonely and afflicted. Relieve the troubles
of my heart and free me from my anguish.*

Psalm 25:16-17

Dear Papa,

I've had parts of this letter floating around in my head since Friday. I don't really want to write it, but it won't leave me alone.

Here's why I dread writing: we sold your business. We sold what you worked on for over fifty years. Since I was a baby you worked on it, and then you handed it off to us and we sold it in three short months. Sure, we kept the land, but we sold the heart and soul of it.

We didn't have a choice. We couldn't do what you thought we could do.

You would hate this sale. Didn't you see it coming, though? Wasn't it one of the things you couldn't ever bring yourself to talk about? So many parts of the business had gotten all knotted and tangled over the last few years. It sure would have been easier if you and I could have untangled it together before you left.

Anyway, a funny thing happened right after the closing. As soon as they told me that all the documents were signed, your cell number popped into my mind. I hadn't thought of it once since you left, but there it was, all of a sudden, front and center. It stays there now, sort of like the ringing in my ears.

I never had that, either, until you left.

There's another new thing, too. Somebody else parks in your spot in front of your office, and I hear that they bought all new furniture. I hope I never see it.

Mom gave me your desk. I like the idea of opening the drawers you used to open and keeping my things where you used to keep your things. Maybe someday I'll learn to clean up the way you did—just sweep the whole mess into the trashcan and start over.

I haven't cried much lately because working on this closing has kept me busy and sort of frozen inside. Ever since the documents were signed, though, I've been making up for lost time.

So many things have happened since you left. It makes me sad that I can't tell you about them. The letters help a little.

Maybe you already know anyway. A lot of people think you can see earth from heaven. They think you watch everything that goes on down here. I'm not so sure. Heaven isn't supposed to have any sorrow or sighing, and I can't understand how anybody could watch things going on down here without being sad—especially you. Either way, I'll probably keep on writing.

I love you.

THE OTHER SIDE OF GRIEF

For I am convinced that neither death nor life ... neither the present nor the future ... will be able to separate us from the love of God that is in Christ Jesus our Lord.

Romans 8:38-39

Dear Papa,

I just got an email from a friend whose father is dying. I have talked to her about you a lot over the years. She says she likes to hear how much we love each other, even though she can't understand it, because her father never loved her. She says that hearing about you and me makes her feel better about the world. I think that's pretty good. If I were in her shoes, I probably would try to find an easier way to feel better about the world.

I went shopping today to buy new khakis for the boys. I was enjoying myself until I remembered that the last time I bought new khakis, they were for you. I didn't find out until we gave your clothes away after the funeral that you had enough pants to open your own store. That's how you were about clothes, though—the more, the merrier.

Clothes and ice cream. With you, it was always time for ice cream. Whenever I suggested it, you would smile that smile and we would head for the ice cream place. You would stand at the counter, leaning forward while I read you the flavor choices, looking like it was a life-or-death decision. When it was time to pay, you would hold out a handful of money like a little boy, and the ice cream lady would count out what she needed and give back the rest. Then we would sit outside in the car, eating ice cream and talking about life like we had all the time in the world.

Remember the little square Italian crackers that I used to send you? The last batch arrived the day before you died, and Mom told you to open it later, after the Easter company left. You left first, though. They served those crackers at the funeral, and I've never bought a box since.

Here's some big news. I bought a car last week. When I was halfway home, it started acting up, and they had to tow it back to the dealer. It reminded me of how you used to tell us that, if we ever got a flat tire, we should just keep on driving. Don't worry about ruining the rims, you'd say. Just keep driving and don't stop until you get someplace safe. Much as you loved your cars, they were junk compared to your girls. I never did drive on the rims, but I always liked knowing you wanted me to.

I took a friend to the hospital today for her radiation treatment. I was sitting in the waiting room doing just fine, and then all of a sudden I started missing you and the tears came again. I had to stand around in the ladies room until they stopped. No one ever knew.

Most people don't know. Sometimes somebody asks me what's wrong, but I don't say much. I can't keep talking about missing you forever. Besides, nothing is really wrong. It's just that, since you left, nothing is quite right.

My friends say that I've gotten too isolated. They say that I need to spend more time with people, and they're probably right. The problem is that, once I'm with people, I can't think of anything to say, and I can't remember how to act. It feels like everything I used to know about being with people disappeared when you did.

Did I ever tell you that, when we sold the business, I took a few tomato plants home with me and planted them in our backyard? One of my friends wants to eat one of the tomatoes together when they ripen, as a little memorial to you, but I don't think I could. With you gone, I've lost my taste for tomatoes, just like I've lost my taste for being with people.

Yet this I call to my mind; and therefore I have hope: Because of the Lord's great love we are not consumed, for His compassions never fail. They are new every morning; great is Your faithfulness.

Lamentations 3:21-23

Dear Papa,

Lately, I've been forgetting to miss you. I've had some normal days. I've been laughing and chatting and even traveling.

I just went to David's father's funeral. I thought that would make me sad all over again, but it didn't. I didn't feel anything really, except sadness for David, because I know where he's headed. Soon, he'll want to call his dad, and then he'll remember that he can't.

The big news is that the tomatoes you planted before you left—the crop we sold—are real beauties. I think this is going to be the blockbuster crop that you hoped for for fifty years.

I keep wondering whether any of this is part of your life now. Mom is convinced that, whenever things go right for her, it's you taking care of her, just like you always did. Who knows?

Your world must be whole now, all clean and pure and clear. It must be fun to wait for us in that shining place.

I dreamed about you last week. It was the first time, really. The other time doesn't count—the time I dreamed that you were walking toward me on the dock, and then, all of a sudden, it wasn't you anymore. This time it really *was* you, and you weren't old anymore. You weren't young, either. You were just solid and good—more you than ever. I knew in the dream that it wouldn't last, and I wanted to stretch the time, to drink in being with you. I guess I did, because when I woke up it didn't hurt.

I've been trying my best to run what's left of your business. You used to say that, if anything ever happened to you, you wanted me to take over. You always said *if* because it sounded so much better than *when*.

Trying to run the business while I'm wading through grief isn't easy. I'm having a hard time keeping my head above water, but I'm doing the best I can. It's my turn now. You did your turn for almost ninety years.

Rest now, my Papa. Breathe easy.

"Though the mountains be shaken and the hills be removed, yet My unfailing love for you will not be shaken nor My covenant of peace removed," says the Lord, who has compassion on you.

Isaiah 54:10

Dear Papa,

I know that writing to you is like playing make-believe. It reminds me of the little girl I saw today in the locker room at the gym, making believe she was a princess. I'm making believe you can hear me.

I'm feeling heavy and stale and stuck these days. I hide it as well as I can, because it has been four months since you left, and even I am beginning to wonder whether something else is wrong with me—something bigger than you being gone.

I might as well let the tears out, though. When I don't, they build up, and I get hard and taut and the kids ask me if I'm mad at them. So today I'll let myself sit here and cry for a while.

I don't think of you as much as I used to. I'm trying to get on with it. The problem is that I never quite know what *it* is anymore. Every once in a while, I get some wind in my sails and start zipping through the day like I used to, but it never lasts. The wind dies down, and I start drifting again.

Most days I have trouble focusing. It's like walking into a room to get something really important, and then realizing that you have no idea what that something is.

These days I can't see beauty in most of the places

I used to see it, but you must see more beauty now than you ever could have imagined. I used to tell you about beautiful heaven-places. Now you live there, and I'm just hanging on down here from one glimpse to another.

You're home now, and I'm on my way. It feels good to remember that again. The tears helped, too. They washed away the dust of trying so hard. Now I can get on with life again, at least for today. I'll worry about tomorrow tomorrow.

My soul is weary with sorrow;
strengthen me according to Your word.

Psalm 119:28

Dear Papa,

I'm afraid of forgetting to remember you. I used to count the Sundays since you left. I would wait for 6:30 Sunday evening and then think about how your cell phone rang just before you had the heart attack and wonder whether you ever knew it was me calling. But now I miss some Sundays, and I don't even realize it until Monday or Tuesday. And sometimes I wake up in the middle of the night and don't even think about you being gone.

The remembering is back today, though. It always comes back whenever there's another first, and today is a first. It's the first time I've ever been in Maine without calling you every day to hear "Hi, my darling." I use to take those words for granted. I didn't realize that they held up a lot of my world.

Sometimes I'm glad you're gone. I'm glad you can't see how they paved the marsh across the creek from your house. I'm glad you can't see your tomatoes growing like gangbusters, just when they're not your tomatoes anymore. And I'm glad you missed yesterday's terrorist attack.

In all these months of remembering things about you, I haven't remembered one cross word. I don't even remember a grumpy word—not toward me, anyway. I know you had a temper at work, but I never saw it. You never brought it home.

You always greeted me like I made your day, and you always looked for ways to make my days easier—little favors and kindnesses that nobody else would have thought of.

You were that way with my children, too. From your side, the view never changed. They said it perfectly at the funeral: "With Papa, you were never just loved. You were adored."

Lately, I've been watching my friend's father. He grimaces and barks, and he hoards everything he has. His heart is shrinking like his body. You got smaller, too, but only on the outside. Inside you were growing fast.

We grew together, especially toward the end. We talked about things that most fathers don't ever talk about with their children. It happened more in the last few years, probably because those were the years when you spent so much of your nighttime praying your shy, I-don't-deserve-it-but-would-you-mind prayers.

I miss you a lot today. The tears came like a storm, and then the children came home. One lay down beside me for a while, until I could start my day again—until I could be part of the family again and do all the things I usually do (except call you).

THE OTHER SIDE OF GRIEF

The Lord is close to the brokenhearted
and saves those who are crushed in spirit.

Psalm 34:18

Dear Papa,

Tuesday is our thirtieth wedding anniversary. You and Mom almost made it to your sixtieth. She and I are going to celebrate your anniversary this year, even though it won't make much sense without you. I guess we'll do what we always do now when we're together—talk about you. We'll bring out all the memories of you that we've been carrying around, and we'll spread them out and sort through them together.

I wish I could tell you that I love you. I wish I could get one of those planes that flies along the beach with banners advertising girlie bars and hair gels. I would fly it as high as I could and make the I-love-you letters huge.

But I guess you don't need planes and banners to tell you about love. You're awash in it now. If I could ask you all over again what's been on your mind lately, you wouldn't need to put on your sunglasses to hide the tears before you answer. I'm the one who needs the sunglasses now. And the plane.

I need the plane today to tell people that my father died and that all the air is leaking out of my world and that I'm having real trouble patching it up. But there is no plane, so I'll just string words together and pull them along behind me. This morning they're heavy, but tomorrow maybe the wind will pick up.

Save me, O God, for the waters
have come up to my neck. I sink in the
miry depths, where there is no foothold. I
have come into the deep waters; the floods
engulf me. I am worn out calling
for help; my throat is parched. My
eyes fail, looking for my God.

Psalm 69:1-3

Dear Papa,

Today I found out about a thousand-year-old book that made my letters to you seem a little less crazy. The book is a conversation between the author and his friend, and you don't realize until the end that his friend is dead. The author just kept right on talking to him like nothing had happened. So we're in good company.

You helped me row this morning. I was out on the river in a skull, and I was getting all rattled and forgetting everything I had learned. The oars were taking on a life of their own. Then I thought about our creek at home when I was little. I thought about you sitting on the dock and me rowing toward you like I used to do. I was little again, and you were waiting again. All of a sudden, rowing was easy. I just thought about rowing toward you—getting closer with every stroke. It was only another kind of make-believe, but it was a good kind.

Mom told me on the phone today that the people we sold your business to have sold over a million boxes of tomatoes already this year. Now I feel even worse about the sale. Anyway, I don't want to hear tomato news anymore unless it's you calling to tell me.

I'm not sure why, but today I keep remembering when you were in the hospital that last time—those miserable, stifling days when you couldn't eat or walk, and you seemed smaller than ever.

One sure thing is that you won't hurt anymore, ever. And you're not small anymore, or weak. No more tears for you. Just mountains of joy. You found what you were looking for, and so one day will I. So one day will I.

He will swallow up death forever.
The Sovereign Lord will wipe away
the tears from all faces.

Isaiah 25:8

Fall 2006

*I often think that the night is more alive
and more richly colored than the day.*

Vincent van Gogh[5]

Dear Papa,

Today is another big milestone. It's the third of September, and you're not here. I have called you every September third for over a decade. We always remember together, and at the end you always say the same thing: "My, my, my." Today I started to learn how to remember without you.

It's scary without you. Before you left, I don't remember being afraid very much, but, since you've been gone, fears seem to pop up everywhere. I'm scared to pursue my career, and I'm scared not to. I'm scared when I wake up in the middle of the night, and I'm scared when I wake up in the morning. I don't even know what I'm afraid of. That's the hard part. I can't pin it down. Maybe I'm afraid of the emptiness— all the blank space.

Sometimes I wonder whether this might be a gift. Now that everything has been erased and I'm staring at a blank canvas, maybe I'll be invited into new ways of thinking about myself and life and other people. I hope so. The old ways sure aren't working too well anymore.

So do not fear, for I am with you; do not be dismayed, for I am your God. I will strengthen you and help you; I will uphold you with My righteous right hand.

Isaiah 41:10

Dear Papa,

I keep asking myself why, even though you've been gone for so many months, I still have trouble sleeping, and the world still seems like such a fear-filled place. Today, I saw at least part of the answer. It's in the book of Genesis—the book of beginnings.

It's the book of beginnings of everything, even grief. In the part I was reading today, it says that the son's soul was bound with his father's soul. Soul bound to soul. That makes sense to me. No wonder my world is falling apart. Since my first breath, my soul has been bound to yours. You were home. You were my safe haven.

There were those middle years when I turned away from you. I was learning that you were human, too, and I kept my distance in silent protest because I still thought too highly of myself. It was in your latter years, when I had fallen down, too, that I came back. We finished father to daughter, friend to friend.

The winter is now past, my Papa. The winter is now past. Flowers have appeared in the land.

THE OTHER SIDE OF GRIEF

*I will lead the blind by ways they have
not known, along unfamiliar paths I will
guide them; I will turn the darkness into
light before them and make the rough
places smooth. These are the things
I will do; I will not forsake them.*

Isaiah 42:16

Dear Papa,

I'm anxious again today, and I can't figure out why. I wonder if it would be the same if you were here.

I can't get used to mornings. Before you left, I always woke up with my thoughts bouncing from one possibility to another, like a child with too many toys. Now there's hardly ever any bouncing. It's more like plodding, one slow step at a time, and reminding myself that I just need to give the day a chance.

Most things seem either scary or boring or both. Take rowing, for example. I've rowed twice this week, and both times I was scared. I pushed through. I did it, and I stayed dry. The first day I was glad afterward, because I had really done something, and the gladness lasted all day, but today's row didn't do that. Today, the world is still flat.

I keep trying, though. I've invited people over for dinner and laughed and talked as if nothing were wrong. The problem is that, when I wake up in the middle of the night, the dark cloud is waiting for me, and I feel small and lonely and inadequate again. So I have to start trying all over again the next day.

I keep thinking that, if I could just get out from

under the pile of undone chores, I would feel better. I bail fast every day, and there's a lot less water in the boat now than there was a month ago, but I don't feel any better about myself or about life. I wonder if I should do some *pro bono* legal work or teach a new class. Maybe then I would get the spark back.

Spark or no spark, I'm being careful about one thing—gratitude. Most days, I rehearse my thanksgivings over and over again. I remind myself that God is close to me while my heart is breaking. That gets me moving at least generally in the right direction.

So here I am, making believe again that I can talk to you and you can hear me. I'm getting ready again to make believe for another family evening that losing you doesn't hurt anymore. Sometimes making believe helps.

For I am afflicted and needy, and my heart is wounded within me.... With my mouth I will give thanks abundantly to the Lord.... For He stands at the right hand of the needy....

Psalm 109:22, 30-31 (NASB)

Dear Papa,

I got up this morning, but I never really woke up—not like I used to wake up. Before you left, I woke up thinking oh-boy-what-should-I-do-first. Now it's just okay-at-least-make-the-coffee.

By noon I couldn't stand it anymore—the nameless, faceless fears, and the tears waiting, and the nagging, relentless reminders of how empty my days are. The weight of it was choking me, so I did something that took all my courage.

I found a place where I could be alone for a long time. I've been scared to do that ever since you left, because what I want most is a break from myself. I want to send myself on vacation for a month and stay here without her. I dreaded being alone, but I finally did it.

Everything came pouring out, just like I was afraid it would. I felt like a lonely, lost child, and it hurt like mad. The tears came in a flood, and then they let up, and then they started all over again. I just let them.

After a while, the tears wore themselves out, and I could finally be really quiet for the first time in a long time. It felt good to rest. And the sun came out.

Somehow, I know again that all is well.

THE OTHER SIDE OF GRIEF

When I said, "My foot is slipping,"
Your unfailing love, Lord, supported
me. When anxiety was great within
me, Your consolation brought me joy.

Psalm 94:18-19

Dear Papa,

I haven't written lately because I've been feeling normal again. We're even having a party in a few weeks. I'm living in the sunshine again. Mostly.

But yesterday, missing you came back like a freight train. All of a sudden I was scared again for no reason at all. I was anxious about everything and nothing in particular. The shortness of breath came back, too—the kind that makes inhaling feel like a full-time job. My ears started ringing again, my appetite left, and the whole world looked gray and felt like it always would. All the things I had been looking forward to doing seemed dull and flat and useless. Free time felt more like a burden than a gift. I just wandered from room to room wondering what to do with myself.

In the end, I did what I always do when grief surfaces, because I've read books on grieving and memorized all the *shoulds*. I exercised. I talked to friends. I prayed. The fear still stuck like glue, and everything still seemed like a waste of time. At night I lay staring at the ceiling, listening to a concert of anxious thoughts against the backdrop of the ringing in my ears. This morning I made it through church and I made it through the kids leaving for the football game. As soon as I was alone, I curled up in bed as small as I could and cried like a baby.

I miss my daddy. No matter how often I remind myself of all the other true things I know, I miss my daddy.

When the missing gets too heavy, my whole body knows it. It's as if the missing-you reservoir gradually fills up until all my body alarms go off. My ears start ringing. I can't sleep. The fears go nuts. Eating a meal feels like climbing Mt. Everest. I don't fight it any more. I'm learning to just go with it. You can't fight city hall.

But now things are okay again. It's Monday morning, and I'm back. The funny (and lonely) thing is that no one even knows I was gone. Now it will be business as usual … until the next train hits.

He was … a man of suffering, and
familiar with pain…. Surely He took
up our pain and bore our suffering.

Isaiah 53:3-4

Dear Papa,

I'm at your house this weekend. I'm sitting in your favorite spot on your porch with the wind and the seagulls. I'm not in your chair, though. Even if I were, it would still be empty.

I came here to write, but, with things still so touch-and-go in my insides, I'm not sure I'll be able to write a word. Oh, well. At least I showed up. That's no small thing these days.

There's still something strange and awful about being in the house where you died. The doctor says it was a sudden thing. He says you had no idea. That's one of my favorite things to remember. You didn't have any time to worry about Mom or the business or who would take care of this place.

I guess this isn't really the spot where you died. It's the spot where you started living.

It is good that you left from here. You were part of this place, and you got your wish—you skipped right over the long hospital stays and the nursing homes, and you left from your favorite spot. It's like Br'er Rabbit and his briar patch.

I never thought I would want to sit here when your chair was empty. I guess I thought that once you were gone all the beauty in this place would slip out after you, but it hasn't. It still feels like home. I'm just looking forward to when the older memories of you grow up and cover the funeral memories, sort of like memory kudzu.

One place I never visit, though, is your grave. They're going to landscape it and put a bench near it and make it a nice place to sit, but I think I'll find somewhere else to go, at least until the kudzu grows.

He has sent Me to
bind up the brokenhearted.

Isaiah 61:1

Dear Papa,

I'll be leaving your house in a few minutes, and I won't get to tell you about how the woodpecker ate his breakfast outside my window this morning. This place you built is still a haven for me. You would like that.

Your room isn't your room anymore, though. It's just a stuffy, empty shell of a place now. I went up there so I could remember you better, but it didn't work.

Once I even tricked myself into walking over to the corner of the property where your grave is. I was taking the dogs on a run, and I stopped for a few minutes, even though it's against my rules. That place doesn't feel like you, either. It's just three bushes and a temporary gravestone that spells your name wrong. From now on, I'll stick to remembering you on the porch on your creek.

You never liked anything that had to do with dying. You wouldn't ever talk about obituaries and gravesites and that kind of thing. But when we used to talk about heaven, you would lean forward in your chair like you were waiting for an ice cream cone. That's when we would talk about the reunions that you would have.

That's when I perk up now, too—when I remember that you and I will have a reunion, too. I was thinking about it just last night, wondering what it will be like. You won't be crooked and slow any more. And there won't be any more goodbyes. Ever.

That's another thing we shared—we both hate goodbyes. I guess I'm glad you're not standing in the driveway like you used to, waving goodbye and hiding the tears behind your sunglasses.

[S]orrowful, yet always rejoicing.

2 Corinthians 6:10

Fall 2006

Dear Papa,

I'm in my little cottage for the day, sitting in the spot you used to love. You used to stare out this window by the hour. I know it was partly because you didn't have much choice after the stroke took away your reading. You hid the embarrassment of it behind jokes, but it must have been hard. Maybe there was a silver lining, though. It gave you all the hours and days of open space for getting to know the God you're with right now.

I wonder whether there is anything like reading in heaven, or whether you already know all the good things there are to know. The fun of reading is seeing new places, taking flights of imagination, and getting lifted out of the mire of the mundane. But up there nothing is mundane, and everything is already lovely and clear and bursting with life. Up there, you can do whatever anyone else can do, because your body is more whole than it ever dreamed of being. I bet you're doing all the things you loved to do down here, only better. Tomatoes must grow like magic.

One of my favorite things is thinking about you without all your regrets. You had collected nine decades of *if-onlys*. It seemed like the older you got, the more you focused on your flaws and rehearsed your mistakes. You would replay all the missed business opportunities and the friendships gone awry and the stroke and the bankruptcy. I think you got smaller in your own eyes toward the end. I hated watching that happen, but now I can see that it made you easier to reach than most people. I guess that's why all the grandchildren loved to be with you, even when there was nothing to talk about. They felt like they were sunbathing.

I wonder whether that's the whole point of all the intertwining of folks on this crazy planet. In the end, when all the dust settles, maybe the whole point is just to be friends—to be gentle enough and brave enough to let each other in. That's what happened with you and me, once I finally forgave you for not being perfect.

So this morning, under the clear fall sky, just short of six months from when you left, I want to say thank you for being my father and my friend. I can look up now. I can see the eagles soaring. At least for this morning, I can love that you're soaring, too. At least for this morning, I can smile for you.

Oh, the comfort — the inexpressible
comfort — of feeling safe with a person,
having neither to weigh thoughts nor measure

words, but pouring them all right out, just as they are, chaff and grain together; certain that a faithful hand will take and sift them, keep what is worth keeping, and then with the breath of kindness blow the rest away.

Dinah Maria Craik[6]

Dear Papa,

It's Sunday night, and I'm alone in the house, missing you to death. I haven't written lately because all the new things that I can't tell you about are just more reminders that you're gone.

Last night, I noticed that we're getting low on firewood. That's when I used to call you, and you would send enough wood for the whole neighborhood.

We're going to your house for Thanksgiving because Mom doesn't want to leave town anymore. The children say it's just as well. They don't want to stay here at our house and see your red Thanksgiving chair sitting empty by the fireplace.

I don't want to start feeling sorry for myself. It's November, and I promised to fill the whole month with thanks. So I'll practice. I hope the feelings catch up soon.

When Thou callest me to go through the dark valley, let me not persuade myself that I know a way round.

John Baillie[7]

Dear Papa,

This afternoon, the morning sunshine seems like a distant memory. Maybe it was the afternoon rain. Or maybe it was seeing that elderly man with eyes like yours. Or maybe it was getting a package from your secretary with two recordings of mine that you had been listening to right before you died.

I don't want to spend the rest of the day telling myself all the things I usually tell myself—that everybody loses parents and that there are plenty of people who have much bigger heartaches than mine. I'm tired of getting caught in that tailspin and, besides, you can't compare heartaches. Telling myself to straighten up and fly right doesn't make the pain go away. It just drives it underground and convinces me to stay busy so that I won't have room for remembering. In the end, it catches up with me anyway. When the busyness wears off, I'm still standing in the same puddles of sadness.

So I thought it might be better this time just to make a cup of tea and write to you and get it all out in the open. I'll let the tears win, at least while nobody else is home. That way maybe I'll feel alive again by dinner. These days, you just never can tell.

THE OTHER SIDE OF GRIEF

*My flesh and my heart may fail, but
God is the strength of my heart and
my portion forever .... I have made
the Sovereign Lord my refuge.*

Psalm 73:26, 28

Dear Papa,

Today was a clear day. I could see for miles. I could finally see that you didn't take all the sparkle with you when you left.

Things are different now because of these healing nights. All alone in the dark, my heart is finding out that I'm not alone. My Father is with me, and He loves me.

Tonight, before I close my eyes, I want to tell you that I can see at least a glimmer of the light that you spend your days in now. If you were still here, I would take you out to lunch and try to tell you about it, but I wouldn't have big enough words, and you would think it was too good to be true anyway.

That's what you always used to say when we talked about heaven, but now you know. Now you see face to face. I guess what I'm trying to say is that I'm starting to see, too.

They rejoice before You as people rejoice at the harvest.

Isaiah 9:3

Dear Papa,

Mom just got home from Houston. She got the good news that you had been waiting for all those years. No more cancer. It's over. You should have been waiting in the driveway to greet her, the way you did so many times when the news was rotten. Now she's bringing her good news back to an empty house.

She told me today that it makes her sad to think about how much you've missed over these past six months. She keeps counting all the things you had been waiting for—things that finally happened right after you left. I told her that we're really the ones who are missing out, not you, but it didn't help either of us very much. Mom felt too small tonight. I could tell. So did I.

Saturday was Veterans' Day. That's the day my boys used to call you to thank you for risking your life for our country. Afterward, you always called me and said, "Isn't it something that those boys remember to call me every single year?" This year we were out of town on Veterans' Day, and that made it easier not to hear my phone ring.

I did pretty well as long as I was away, but, as soon as I got home, the storm of missing you hit again. I was going through the bills and Christmas catalogs that had stacked up while I was gone, and there was something from Hospice about how to grieve well—spend time alone, spend time with people who love you, and do things that give you pleasure, even though you probably won't really enjoy them. It says life might feel meaningless sometimes, but it won't always be that way.

I know it won't, but I sure am having trouble tonight remembering what I used to do when I used to get home from trips. I know there are still good things. They're just hiding for a while under this pile of hurt.

If I say, "Surely the darkness will hide me and the light become night around me," even the darkness will not be dark to You; the night will shine like the day, for darkness is as light to You.

Psalm 139:11-12

Dear Papa,

It happened again today. I was zipping through the day, and then I got blindsided. I was at the gym, and an elderly man walked in. He had a kind smile like yours, and he moved slowly like you used to move. I wanted to ask if I could go home with him and sit with him and listen to his stories. I wanted him to be you. Not that I want you back here. He had a walker, and his wife was driving him, and I bet he hates that like you would have hated it.

I'm glad that you're whole now, but being glad for you doesn't stop the tears. I've tried reasoning with them, but they just keep coming back. So I let them. We're getting to be friends.

Here's the problem: tomorrow is Thanksgiving, and you should be here. I keep thinking about that Thanksgiving a few years ago when you wanted to stay up late talking by the fire, and I went to bed and left Jane to talk to you. I'd give anything to have a do-over for that night.

The house feels so empty now. I still want to be cooking and waiting for you and Mom to get here and hearing you say how amazing it is that I can cook a feast without looking like I'm trying. I want to wander through the produce section at the grocery store like we always did, saying how we can't believe what people will pay these days for a few tomatoes.

I can't wait to join you where good things don't end— where right-now makes memories seem pale and thin, instead of the other way around.

Having you in heaven gives me a whole new world to wonder about. I don't want to go there yet, but I wouldn't mind a visit, just to get a glimpse of you all shining and strong. For now, I want to be here in the most solid and good way I can. I want to love the people I love here with my whole heart, even with the broken parts —maybe especially with the broken parts.

Bring my soul out of prison, so
that I may give thanks...

Psalm 142:7 (NASB)

Dear Papa,

We're going out to the country to cut a Christmas tree today. I think the part you always liked best about the tree-cutting trips was the kids telling us that, when they have families, they're going to buy their Christmas trees at the nearest gas station instead of wasting a whole day in the country. You always thought that was a riot.

I would give a whole lot to have you in the back seat today, but a friend told me something recently that helps me not feel so empty about it. She said that you're still loving us, even though you feel so gone. And why not? Why would love get smaller in its native land? I hope mine grows and grows so that when I see you again my eyes will be used to the light.

You loved me here for fifty-four years, and your love still waters every nook and cranny of my world. Your love taught me to be loved. After all the years of saying yes to your love, it was like rolling off a log to say yes to the love pouring down from heaven.

I guess I'm just saying the same thing I always say—thank you. I went through most of my life feeling safe and sure because your love always helped me keep my balance. I never knew until you left that I still had the training wheels on, but I can sure tell now. Without them, I'm wobbling and lurching all over the place.

As a father has compassion on his children, so the Lord has compassion on those who revere Him.

Psalm 103:13

Dear Papa,

You and I talked a lot those last few years about being thankful no matter what. I would send you recordings about it, and you would listen to them over and over again. Somebody put white finger-nail polish on the 'play' button so you would know which one to push.

You lived gratitude toward the end. When we were sitting in that awful hospital room the month before you died, I finally scraped together enough courage to ask you how you were doing. You said you had been listening to the gratitude recordings a lot before you got sick, and you said you were fine. I know there was pain and fear mixed up in that "fine," but I think you meant the deepest part of it.

Mom is fine, too, mostly because of you. When-ever anything good happens now, she says it's you still taking good care of her. I called her a few days ago to tell her some good news, and she said what she always says: "It's Daddy."

It's Daddy. That kind of says it all. *It's Daddy* weaves in and out of all my days. It always has and it probably always will, but it feels different now than it did a few months ago. Instead of being something to get rid of or put behind me, it's something to treasure and learn from and keep company with. It's part of me.

When you first left, I read books about grieving, and I went to a group about grieving, and I talked to people who knew about grieving. I think one of the main things I wanted to find out was how much longer. How much longer will it hurt like this? How much longer until I feel like my old self again? How much longer until I can get back to business as usual?

This morning I know the answer. Forever. That's how much longer.

Return to your rest, my soul, for the Lord has been good to you. For you, Lord, have delivered me from death, my eyes from tears, my feet from stumbling.

Psalm 116:7-8

Winter 2006 – 2007

When Jesus tells us about his Father, we distrust him. When he shows us his Home, we turn away, but when he confides to us that he is "acquainted with grief," we listen, for that also is an acquaintance of our own.

Emily Dickinson[8]

THE OTHER SIDE OF GRIEF

Dear Papa,

It's snowing hard. I was out walking in the snow just after the sun came up. I wanted to call you and tell you how the little stream is starting to fill up with snow and how we can hardly see the path we shoveled last night. I miss loving snow with you.

When we were little, I remember how you used to tie our saucer sleds to the back of your tractor and pull us around the pasture. Sometimes you'd pull us around the edges of the fields, so that our sleds would slide down the creek bank into the frozen marsh and then zip back up again. I never knew it was anything special. I thought it was just what people did in the snow.

No matter how old you got, you always hoped for snow. Most people dread snow because they think of all the things they won't be able to do in it. Not you. The more it snowed, the better you liked it. You'd just sit and watch and smile.

I know now that you weren't just watching the snow. You were watching the way things used to be in the snow. That's how I'm watching it this morning. I keep seeing my kids when they were little, all bundled up and sledding down our hill, and the little boots and mittens drying by the woodstove and the hot chocolate and the snow cream.

And you, my Papa? What are you watching today in your shining place? Someday I'll watch with you, but today is a good earth day, and I have to put away this heavy heart before the others wake up.

Tears have watered the dawn, and I will fill the rest of the day with thanks. I will choose a grateful heart. I will remember you today, and I will remember that one day all tears will be tears of joy.

Gladness and joy will overtake them, and sorrow and sighing will flee away.

Isaiah 35:10

Dear Papa,

You would love this clean, quiet early morning. You've seen more early mornings than anyone else I know. How many mornings did you spend alone like this, I wonder, soaking in the beauty? Mostly I remember hearing the crunch of your tires on the driveway gravel through the fog of sleep, but happily there were mornings when I hopped out of bed and went to work with you. I would trade many hours of sleep now for one of those mornings together.

They seemed so unremarkable at the time. I would stand outside your office with you while you stood around with your foremen. You and your men would stare at the ground, kicking the occasional stone. Every once in a while, somebody would say a few words, and then you'd all look down again and shift from foot to foot. Somehow, out of all that kicking and shuffling, everybody figured out what they were supposed to do that day. They were ready to farm. It was a man's world.

When we headed to the fields, it was different. You would leave the business of farming behind. I can see you now, squatting down to look at the young tomato plants. You'd stroke the leaves like a proud parent and say how pretty they were.

People say that you may have been the best tomato farmer on the east coast. I don't know about that. All I know is that I'm glad I got out of bed a handful of times to watch you do it.

I guess my love for plants comes from you. Plants are good company. Even when they get all raggedy and hopeless, I can hardly stand to get rid of them. Sometimes they just need to rest in the sun for a while.

That's what I'm doing this morning—resting for a while, thinking about you and letting the missing you put down some new roots.

My God turns my darkness into light.

Psalm 18:28

Dear Papa,

Here's a tale that you would have loved. At the Christmas party, I forgot to move the cat food off the piano, and a few people thought it was an appetizer. I wish I could have called you the next morning. We would have laughed our heads off. And then, every few months afterwards, we would have pulled that story back out and laughed like we had never heard it before.

For a long time after you left, I quit laughing. The best I could do was a make-believe laugh so that I wouldn't stand out too much in a crowd. But things are different now. I can even look at your photo on my office wall and say good morning to you without crying. Maybe just for fun I'll tell you the cat story anyway.

At midnight I rise to give You thanks.

Psalm 119:62

Dear Papa,

It's been a long time since I've written. I hardly know where to start.

I've been sick. It only lasted a week, but it felt like forever. I wonder, if you were still here, how many times you would have called me. If it were ten years ago, you'd have shown up on my doorstep.

I remember the time you did that. You drove four hours from your house to ours, had a cup of coffee in the kitchen, and then drove four hours back—just for the pleasure of our company.

I guess I learned that from you, because I used to drive down from Washington to surprise you, too. I'd come sashaying into your office, and your whole day would light up. Everybody at the office knew it, and so did I.

There aren't many people whose worlds light up just because you walk into the room. You were one for me, and I was one for you.

Mom was brave at Christmas. Nobody knew how to act without you, so she broke the ice. She told funny stories about you from a long time ago. She has a whole heart full of them.

She and I talked beforehand about who would wear your red jacket on Christmas Eve. It's hanging in your closet all by itself. Christmas came and went, and it's still hanging there. I guess that answers the question.

A few weeks later, a lady at a party asked me how I was doing, and I told her that it's been a hard year because my father died. She said her father died, too, and then she started to cry, right there in the middle of the cocktails. She had to look away until she could collect herself. I said, "I'm sorry. How long ago did he die?"

"Twenty-three years," she said.

Twenty-three years is a lot more than nine months. I'm glad she cried. It told me that I don't have to get over losing you, like people get over having the flu. I can keep carrying you in my heart, and if somebody asks me about you at a cocktail party twenty-three years from now, I can cry, too, without saying how silly of me.

[T]he Father of compassion and the God of all comfort, who comforts us in all our troubles, so that we can comfort those in any trouble with the comfort we ourselves receive from God.

2 Corinthians 1:3-4

Dear Papa,

It's my birthday. I've never had a birthday without you before, and it isn't easy.

The children surprised me with an album full of letters from friends. Some things people wrote surprised me because I hadn't known what I meant to them. With you, I always knew. You told me all the time, even when you didn't say a word.

Today is the first day I've really missed you in a long, long time. That surprises me, but then this whole year without you has been one surprise after another.

For a long time, every day was a struggle, and then, right after Christmas, all of a sudden it was smooth sailing. I started doing all the things I used to do, and it felt normal, as if all the months of hurting were somebody else's pain. There were no more rogue tears. There was no more slogging through hours that hardly seemed to budge. It was as if somebody flipped a magic switch and, just like that, I could live without you.

But today is different. The tears are back again. I could feel them collecting all afternoon. I tried to ignore them because it's my birthday, but then I realized that the tears meant it would be a letter-writing day, and I was glad. The truth is, it feels good to be missing you again.

I never want to have a birthday without you, even if it hurts. The tears are good. They wash all the dust off my memory of you. It's all clear now, as if you might call any minute.

O Joy that seekest me through pain
I cannot close my heart to Thee
I trace the rainbow through the rain
and feel the promise is not vain
that morn shall tearless be.

George Matheson[9]

Spring 2007

It is in the dark that God is passing by.
The bridge and our lives shake not because
God has abandoned, but the exact
opposite: God is passing by. God is in the
tremors. Dark is the holiest ground.... In
the blackest, God is closest, at work,
forging His perfect and right will. Though
it is black and we can't see and our world
seems to be free-falling and we feel utterly
alone, Christ is most present to us....

Ann Voskamp[10]

Dear Papa,

Happy birthday to you. I'm driving home to be with Mom so we can celebrate together.

We're finally getting your permanent headstone put in place. We tried a few months ago, but the ground was too frozen. I don't care much about it, but for Mom it's a good remembering place, especially since she can see it from her bedroom window.

There are two things you would like about it—it's close to your creek, and the engraving on it says that you fought in the war.

A few days ago, I was talking to a friend about her dad. He can't carry on a conversation anymore, and often he doesn't know who she is. He watches TV all day without really seeing it. He spends his days just staring at the screen. Leaving all of a sudden like you did seems a whole lot better than leaving little by little. I'm glad you went home fast.

THE OTHER SIDE OF GRIEF

Think not thou canst sigh a sigh
And thy Maker is not by;
Think not thou canst weep a tear
And thy Maker is not near...
Till our grief is fled and gone
He doth sit by us and moan.

William Blake[11]

Dear Papa,

I didn't even know it was time to plant tomatoes until the man who bought your business told
me. That's a first. You and I used to talk all winter
about the spring planting. It was the day you looked
forward to most—the day that marked the end of
the long months of doing nothing, especially after
your stroke.

You always turned into an old man during the
winter and then you got young again when the
spring planting started. You did it again last year.
You were in the hospital dying in February, and in
March you were showing me the baby tomato plants
in the greenhouses.

But this year you're gone, and the day of spring
planting sneaked up on me. I was on the phone with
the new owner, telling him that we need to finalize
some leases, and he said, "We're planting tomorrow, Betsy." The tears came before I could hang up.

Funny, just an hour ago a friend asked me if I had
been missing you a lot lately, and I said no. I had
no idea that I'd be crumpled up in my desk chair
crying again this afternoon.

But it's different now. It's not that awful, empty,
black kind of missing you—the kind that drains the

whole world of color. This is a softer, kinder sadness. The storms still come, but they go, too, and the sun comes back out.

I'm glad that you could work right up until your very last day. You didn't die in your fields, but you only missed by a few hours. You spent your last afternoon looking at your tomato plants and visiting with family. And then you left.

Most people only have one day a year that marks their leaving, but you have two. Two days every April will always be the days Papa died. There's Easter Sunday, and that's good because it's all about resurrection and new life and family being together. And then there's April 16th, and that's good, too, because it will be my quiet, private remembering day.

I never made it to the zoo on my birthday this year, so maybe I'll go on April 16th. Maybe that can be my remembering place, there with the animals. You would like that. You liked animals almost as much as you liked tomatoes and ice cream.

Weeping may stay for the night, but
rejoicing comes in the morning.

Psalm 30:5

Dear Papa,

I miss you again tonight. I watched a movie, and for two hours I completely forgot you were gone. The sudden rememberings are the worst ones.

I can't wait to get my new books about heaven so I can imagine better where you are and all the fun you're having.

I know that I'll see you again, but missing you still hurts. I'm trying hard. I'm trying to remember all the true things, but every once in a while the dam breaks.

I wish I had more things that used to be yours. I wish I could think of some small thing that nobody else would want—something I could hold when my heart hurts. I wish I had recorded some of our conversations like I always intended to. I guess I just wish you hadn't left, and the wishing comes out in a thousand small *if-onlys*.

Low-sunk life imagines itself weary of life,
but it is death, not life, it is weary of.

George MacDonald[12]

Spring 2008

And you come through. It's like having a
broken leg that never heals perfectly—that
still hurts when the weather gets cold,
but you learn to dance with the limp.

Anne Lamott[13]

Dear Papa,

It's your birthday again. At first, I was caught between tears and not remembering. Part of me wanted to just remember you in passing. I was afraid of feeling all the pain of missing you again, and I was even more afraid of having no tears at all. I took the risk of remembering. I came heart in hand.

In church this morning, we sang about heaven, and I imagined you at home in all that joy. The tears came afterwards, but they were happy tears. They left me wrapped in warmth and goodness. I guess that's because I got a little glimpse of your land of light. You're home, and I'm on my way. What more can I ask?

Grief melts away
Like snow in May,
As if there were no such cold thing.

George Herbert[14]

Dear Papa,

I don't know if I can write this letter. It may be too late. Last night was the right time, but I was driving, and it was all I could do to see the road through the tears.

The grief hit out of the blue again. There was no warning at all. I should have known, though. I should have known that going to your best friend's funeral would bring back my missing you.

We were sitting in the church, waiting for the service to start, and your friend Buddy Thatch sat down right behind us. His eyes are just like yours, all kind and eager and soft. Then, during one of the eulogies, somebody mentioned your name. "And his good friend, Carlton Byrd…." Before I could prepare myself for the onslaught, the last two years melted away, and in a heartbeat my whole world was filled again with one, huge, screaming fact—that my good friend Carlton Byrd isn't here anymore.

I had to leave early, and I cried halfway back to Washington. Once the tears started, everything came tumbling out. For so long, I had been collecting all the things that I wanted to tell you about, shoving them all into some back part of my heart like I toss odds and ends into the foyer closet until I can hardly get the door shut. Somehow the funeral opened the door, and everything fell out all over the place.

One thing I've wanted to tell you is that we have owls living in our backyard. I hear them calling to each other all day long, and I wonder why. Aren't owls supposed to be night creatures? You and I would have wondered together, wouldn't we? And then we would have talked about when you last saw the wild turkeys in your field. I hardly ever see them now that you're gone. Maybe that's because you're not here anymore to stop people from shooting them.

It hurts that there is so much I haven't been able to tell you. The owls are just the tip of the iceberg. The longer you're gone, the bigger the pile gets. I know I can tell other people, but it's not the same somehow.

Even after a good night's sleep, I can't seem to shake the sadness. It makes me too heavy to be with people. It feels the way it felt during the first months after you left—like the laughter is gone for good. And things seem sort of pointless again—refinishing the table; doing the wash; even writing. Bigger things, like business, seem out of reach anyway because I'm so tired. I'm not tired, really, but weary—as if the simplest things take more energy than I can scrape together. I don't have much appetite, either. I just eat because it's time to—or I don't. And it's hard to take a good, deep breath.

These are all familiar things. I lived with them for months after you left, but I thought I had said goodbye to them for good. I thought that the empty place you left was finally filling up, but now I know it was just kind of wallpapered over.

Everybody says this is how grief behaves. It's not very polite. It doesn't knock.

Maybe I shouldn't fight it. Maybe I should just say thank you for the chance to remember again, even if it means feeling all the pain again, too.

Maybe I should give myself a break today and not expect too much, like I do when I have the flu. Come to think of it, this is sort of like having the flu. Being fifty-six and wanting your daddy makes you feel sick, and saying that it shouldn't only makes things worse.

I love you.

When I can no more stir my soul to move,
And life is but the ashes of a fire;
When I can but remember that my heart
Once used to live and love, long and aspire --
Oh, be thou then the first, the one thou art;
Be thou the calling, before all answering love,
And in me wake hope, fear, boundless desire.

George MacDonald[15]

Dear Papa,

I don't think much about writing to you anymore. It's so different now. I go through whole days and sometimes even weeks without thinking of you much at all, and then I'm surprised when I remember. I used to be so afraid of forgetting you, but now I'm not. Maybe that's because we'll know each other much better in heaven than we ever knew each other here.

When I do remember you now, the remembering comes out of nowhere. It happened last week. I was sipping my morning coffee, and I flipped to a psalm about being scared and needing help and how God comes to the rescue. It made perfect sense to me, the way so much of His love makes sense to me. It makes sense because that's the way you were.

I read that psalm, and all of a sudden I was twelve again. You were working late at your office, and Clare and I were at home, munching on popcorn and watching the Miss America pageant. We heard footsteps. Nobody else was home, and home was miles from anywhere. So we did what we always did when we were in any kind of trouble. We called you. Soon we heard your car racing down the driveway— the sound of you rescuing us, like you always did.

THE OTHER SIDE OF GRIEF

*He drew me out of deep waters. He
rescued me from my powerful enemy, ...He
rescued me because He delighted in me.*

Psalm 18:16-17, 19

Dear Papa,

I just got the call—the lawsuit about your business is finally over. It ended today, April 16, exactly two years from the day you left. I wanted to be at your house so I could celebrate on your porch in the dark with just the stars around, but I had to settle for the hammock here under our hemlock tree.

I'm glad that your remembering day is April 16, because it's your favorite time of year. It's spring planting time.

I haven't seen the owls yet this spring. I'm afraid they might have moved, but I keep the binoculars on my desk, just in case.

That reminds me of Little Domore. Did I ever tell you that she died? It seems funny around here without a cat. I'll never forget the day we got our first two cats. The children were in the back seat with the kittens on their laps, and we bumped into you near Truman's store. You leaned on our car and watched the kids watching the kittens, and then you gave me that seal-of-approval look.

I lived with that look for so many years that learning to live without it almost killed me. Thank you, my fine Papa.

THE OTHER SIDE OF GRIEF

*He heals the brokenhearted and
binds up their wounds.*

Psalm 147:3

Summer 2008

*The great challenge is living your wounds through
instead of thinking them through. It is better to cry
than to worry, better to feel your wounds deeply
than to understand them, better to let them enter
into your silence than to talk about them. The
choice you face constantly is whether you are taking
your hurts to your head or to your heart. In your
head you can analyze them, find their causes and
consequences, and coin words to speak and write
about them. But no final healing is likely to come
from that source. You need to let your wounds
go down into your heart. Then you can live them
through and discover that they will not destroy
you. Your heart is greater than your wounds.*

Henry Nouwen[16]

Dear Papa,

I said goodbye to Wray and the boys this morning. They're on their way to Alaska for adventure, and I feel sick because every goodbye brings back the goodbye to you that I've said over and over again. I guess I'll keep on saying it until I see you again.

It occurred to me on the way home from the airport that you were bad at goodbyes, too. I can still see you standing in the driveway waving goodbye to us and making believe you weren't crying. We always knew. Everybody knew. Your goodbye hugs always broke my heart. I guess some folks like goodbyes because sometimes they lead to adventures, but I feel the same way you did about them. No matter what adventure might come later, you have to leave somebody behind first to get there.

Whenever we were all at your house together, you always joked about closing the gate at the end of the driveway so nobody could leave. I know what you mean now. If I had had a gate this morning, I would have wanted it closed and locked.

I want heaven. I'm sure that in heaven you can have adventures without ever having a huge empty space between your heart and somebody else's.

There are no more goodbyes for you. There's no more missing people. For you, it's all hellos and laughter and adventure and sameness, all at once. It's part of heaven magic.

I love you, my Papa.

Rise, heart; thy Lord is risen.

George Herbert[17]

Dear Papa,

I went to your house this weekend with some friends. I could feel the missing you filling up my insides, and I didn't want it to come out in front of people. It's not that I was embarrassed. I just wanted to miss you by myself. So I went grocery shopping. As soon as I was in the car, the tears came, and here they are again.

I drove past your field and saw all the deer and thought how you and I would have stopped and enjoyed them together. You would have said how beautiful they were. Or, better yet, you wouldn't have said anything at all. It's just not the same watching them alone.

When I got to town, there was an old man selling tomatoes out of the back of his truck. I told him that my father Carlton Byrd used to grow tomatoes, and he said he knew Carlton Byrd. I told him how much I miss you, and he said everybody misses Carlton Byrd because Carlton Byrd was *The Man*. I wanted him to talk more about you, but I guess he wasn't in the mood, so I left and cried my way through the grocery store.

Sometimes I wonder whether it's wrong to still be crying. Since you left, I've watched friend after friend say goodbye to parents. I always wait on the sidelines, ready to help them get back on their feet, but after a few months they seem okay, and I'm the only one still crying.

Anytime I try to figure that out, I end up either making them wrong or making myself wrong. It's a losing battle. Deep down, I know the answer. We're all different, and our hearts ache differently. At least for this morning, I won't try to make my grief look like somebody else's or squeeze it into somebody else's timeline. And I won't try to hold back the tears just because nobody else is still crying. I'll let myself feel the hurt and the missing you without dissecting it.

I miss you, Papa. I just plain miss you. I know the tears will stop soon and the air will be crisp again. I'll laugh again and remember again that you are safe and whole and laughing again. But not yet. Not yet.

Yet I am not alone,
for my Father is with Me.

John 16:32

Fall and Winter 2008 – 2009

After a while, though the grief did not go away from us, it grew quiet. What had seemed a storm wailing through the entire darkness seemed to come in at last and lie down.

Wendell Berry[18]

Dear Papa,

I dreamed about you last night. You were holding a baby, and you kept looking from the baby to
me and back again. The funny thing was that it felt
so natural, like you had never been away. It was
the opposite of the way people act when they've
been away from each other for a long time—running toward each other, hugging, staring, hugging
some more, smiling, and both talking at once to
try to catch up. Now that I think of it, no one said
anything in the dream. We were just there.

You were different. I didn't realize it during the
dream, though, because in a strange way you seemed
more like yourself than you ever had been before.
The wistful part of you—the tentative part, the part
that dreaded goodbyes—was gone. It was as if you
had found everything you were looking for, and you
were more solid than ever.

I didn't notice what you looked like. I can't

remember whether you looked young or old. Both, I think. It was your eyes that mattered. They looked straight into mine. And when you looked away, it wasn't because you were self-conscious and needed a break. I guess in heaven closeness isn't embarrassing anymore.

I've been glad ever since I woke up. I thought the dream would bring back the old longings or even make them worse, but it didn't. It just gave me more to look forward to, and it reminded me that you don't belong here anymore. You've outgrown the old you, but not in a way that makes me feel like you've outgrown me, too. You only outgrew the earth things—the things that make people sad and lonely.

You're whole now, my Papa. No more worries. No more *if-onlys*. A dream come true.

When we meet our beloved in Him, we shall both know and love them as we have neither loved nor known before.

Henry E. Manning[19]

Dear Papa,

I got blindsided by the tears again today. It was the first time in a long time, and it hit right in the middle of the workday.

One of the children called with good news. That's when I always used to pick up the phone and call you, and that's what I wanted to do today. We would have talked about this piece of good news up one side and down the other. One of the things I loved about you was that our children were like your children. Their news was your news.

I remember when Chess was six and you took her to the hair salon down the street to have her hair washed and dried. I thought it was a waste of money, but you knew just what you were doing. You were letting her feel like a princess.

I remember when you took her to Baskin Robbins and told her to order whatever she wanted. She got so many scoops that they had to give her a bowl to catch the ones that fell off the cone. You sat there for over an hour watching her. She still talks about it. She still can't believe that you gave her all the time and ice cream in the world.

I remember how, after your stroke, you sent the children cash when they were teenagers. You wrote notes on yellow Post-it notes. We still have those notes, and we still can't read them. That doesn't matter. We all knew what they said.

I loved that you never quit trying to learn to read and write again after your stroke. I remember how you would take the *Wall Street Journal* up to your room every morning and stay there as long as it took to fight your way through one front-page article. You always came back downstairs with a splitting headache, but you never quit.

You never quit in business either. I remember the day I sat beside you on your office couch and told you there was no way around the bankruptcy. You sat there with your spring planting lists in one hand and my hand in the other. You kept saying, "But it's almost time to plant."

Every time you got a new crop in the ground, you came to life again, just like Popeye after he ate his spinach. And you did it that year, too. You planted in spite of us. You planted your way right through the bankruptcy and out the other end. You beat the odds. I love remembering that.

The remembering feels good today. The tears are a relief after all the dry months. And it's a relief to know that the letters aren't over. Maybe they'll never quit, just like you never quit. They're gifts out of the blue.

Fall and Winter 2008–2009

You will fill me with joy in Your presence.

Psalm 16:11

Dear Papa,

I got caught off guard again. I was on the phone with your credit card company. I was in my can-do, check-it-off-the-list mode, but I didn't get very far. The man from the credit card company kept asking me questions that I couldn't answer.

"When did your father pass? Ma'am? Are you still there? We need to know the date of death."

I wanted to say, *Yes, I'm still here, but I can't answer you right now—not without crying, anyway. I know what the date is. It's seared into my soul. But I can't get the words out.*

"Ma'am, we need you to verify some information for us so that we can remove the deceased from the account. When did he pass?"

I wanted to say, *Well, that's what I'm trying to tell you. You think it just happened, and so do I sometimes. But it didn't just happen. It was almost three-and-a-half years ago, but some days I still have trouble getting used to the idea.*

"Ma'am, you want us to take your father's name off the card and make your mother the primary, right? Ma'am? Are you there?"

I wanted to say, *Sort of. I mean, part of me is, but a lot of me still keeps slipping backwards and thinking about how many things I want to tell him, especially since today is September third again.*

"I'm sorry for your loss, Ma'am."

Me, too. Again. Just when I thought I had this thing down. It just goes to show, you never can tell.

O Lord, when I do think of my departed, I think of Thee, who art the death of parting.

George MacDonald[20]

Photograph by Francesca Fitch

Reflections on Grief

The heart has its reasons that reason knows not of.

Blaise Pascal[21]

Grief is a wild and mysterious thing. It swept me up and carried me in its current while I tried with every desperate shred of strength I had to get back to shore. For a long, long time, I got dragged downstream, hitting rocks and getting caught in currents that pulled me under for longer than I thought I could stand.

For a long time, grief felt dead and barren and hopeless, but it ushered me into new freedom and deeper joy and broader vistas than I had ever known before. I learned that grief can bear good fruit.

I have seen that good fruit in abundance in the life of my friend Barbara. She has multiple sclerosis. It struck almost two decades ago, when she had four young children. She never knows from day to day whether she will be able to sit up or speak or even smile. She spends many days in bed in excruciating pain, but she has chosen to view her sickness as a gateway rather than as a limitation. She calls it God's private tutorial. She knows that He could take the disease away in the blink of an eye, so, until He does, she embraces it with an open heart, eager to learn everything that He has to teach her. She lives gratefully, and she is the healthiest, most contented and joy-filled person I've ever known.

Most people in Barbara's situation would be hard and bitter and self-focused. Their worlds would have shrunk over the years of pain. Hers has expanded. She loves more, and more freely, than anyone else I know. It is no coincidence that she also has suffered more than anyone else I know.

Sooner or later, grief comes to everybody.[22] You can't avoid painful circumstances, but you can choose how you're going to react to them. Basically, that means choosing where you will hide, because when you're in pain, you *will* hide. It's not very complicated because there are only two choices: you either turn, little by little, to God and throw the whole weight of your grief on Him, or you turn, little by little, to yourself and whatever hiding places you can create.

I understand why a lot of people choose to create their own hiding places. In the short run, it's a lot faster and easier. You buck up and play the stoic. You lecture yourself on all the *shoulds.* You tell yourself not to be a baby. You shove the pain down. You hide from it in busyness or in the next drink or in somebody else, and, for a while, that seems to work.

For a while, it keeps the pain at bay.

Eventually, though, grief finds its way out. If you lock the door, it slides under. It comes out in disguise—in things like headaches and anger and depression and broken relationships and loss of heart. If you refuse to feel the grief, you get sick in body or soul or mind or heart.

A friend told me that she has been too busy for the past two years to grieve her father's death. In the next breath, she said, "It's the oddest thing. I've gained thirty-five pounds since he died. I've never been this heavy in my life." Exactly.

In the long run, choosing to create your own hiding places doesn't work. It puts all the pressure on you to keep life running smoothly and to keep the pain buried. To do that, you have to be self-focused and self-protective. You can't afford to get too close to people because, in the light of friendship, the pain that you've worked so hard to bury just might surface. You have to be especially guarded around people who are in pain themselves, because their pain, if you get too close, might unearth yours. So you have to stay near the surface with people.

You have to stay near the surface with God, too. You have to be sure that the place in your heart where all the pain is buried stays closed and locked, so you can't let your guard down with God, either. Prayer will be, at best, a polite affair.

Your heart will be like the lone cowboy, staring out at the horizon. That might look appealing in the movies, but, in real life, me-myself-and-I is lonely company.

God hates to see us choose that company. He didn't create us to be loners. He created us to live together, heart to heart, but we can't do that unless He frees us from all the self-focus and self-enclosure that keeps us isolated from each other. That's why He keeps knocking and calling.[23]

Knocking and calling.... What if the very things we dread most—the heart-stopping phone call, the diagnosis, the divorce, losing someone we love—are God knocking? It's a radical way of seeing pain, I know. I'm not saying that the bad things themselves are good. They're not. Cancer isn't good, and neither is divorce or death or getting fired. But *God* is good, and He can take the grief that comes in the wake of those bad things and work His miracles in the midst of it all. He can bring order out of the chaos. He can turn darkness into light. He can create new life out of what looks dead and hopeless. That's exactly what He does if you have the courage to grieve well.

Grieving well does take courage—maybe more courage than anything else you will ever do. Facing the pain instead of burying it takes courage, and the deeper the pain and the more it devastates, the more courage you will need. The big temptation is to focus all your attention on one burning question: *How can I get out of this pain?*

It's the wrong question, but it's the question that our culture encourages you to ask. Modern life is no friend to grief. It sees grief as a waste of time. It wants grief to disappear—and the faster, the better.

Modern culture has unspoken rules, and grief breaks every one of them. You're supposed to move fast, and grief is agonizingly slow. You're supposed to be efficient and productive, and grief is about as far as you will ever get from efficiency and neatness and airtight explanations and what most people refer to as "progress."

In fact, grief usually looks and feels more like regress than progress. You can't do the things that you used to be able to do easily. You're not sure of anything anymore—especially yourself. On the darkest days, you hardly recognize yourself, and sometimes you're afraid that you never will. Grief makes you feel like you're falling apart, and falling apart isn't exactly our idea of progress. So grief has to go underground. You learn to hide it, sometimes even from yourself.

For one thing, grief makes most people uncomfortable. The unspoken message is that, after a few weeks or at most a few months, you really should get back on your feet and get on with life. Hardly anyone comes right out and says that, but you can see it in their eyes, and you can hear it in what they don't say. As author Michael Casey says,

> In the culture of the industrialized Western world…we are led to expect that [suffering] should not occur…. We come to believe it is not right to experience pain. We are encouraged to block it out, to forget our misery, to act 'normally.' Millions of people walk around pretending to be 'normal.'[24]

There are a lot of reasons for this. On a purely practical level, grief is inconvenient. When you are too incapacitated to do what you used to do at the office or at home or wherever, things fall through the cracks, and other people have to cover for you. It means more work for them. Besides, people around you feel your pain, and most of them don't like that. They don't need more pain. They have plenty of their own.

There is also a deeper dynamic. The fallout of grief scares people. If people see you so thoroughly undone by grief, that means it could happen to them, too. That puts front-and-center the very question that most people are trying hard not to ask: *Is my life built on sand or rock?* Most people don't really want to know the answer to that question, so most of the time most of us walk around pretending that we're fine.

We pretend by creating functional identities—by making believe that I am what I do and you are what you do. Your identity becomes what you do at work and what you do on your days off and whose husband or wife or friend you are. So you *are* how well you play tennis, how many witty comments you can make, how much money you earn, and how well you help other people. You *are* what you *do*.

That functional identity works pretty well until grief hits like a freight train, and all of a sudden you can't *do* much of anything. The pain shatters this fragile functional identity like a mirror, and you're left staring down at the broken glass around your feet. I know, because it happened to me.

At this point, part of me wishes that I had a really dramatic story to tell you about the terrible thing that caused my life to derail—something that would cause you to say, "Wow, no wonder she fell apart." But I don't have a dramatic story. In fact, while you were reading my letters to Papa, you might have wondered from time to time whether something is wrong with me because the size of the loss doesn't seem to warrant the extent of the damage. After all, he was old and he had a good life and everybody's parents die. I couldn't agree more, but it didn't matter. All the *shoulds* in the world couldn't get my heart to shape up.

No matter how much I told myself that I *should* be getting better, I kept getting worse. I was shocked. I had spent decades putting myself together, organizing my life, getting things on an even keel, and then, all of a sudden, everything changed.

Before Papa died, I was an energetic, upbeat, let-me-help-you kind of person. After he died, I could hardly put one foot in front of the other. I went from speaking at large conferences to hiding when the doorbell rang.

I avoided people, mostly because I couldn't remember how to act around them. I couldn't think of anything to say, and, when they laughed, I couldn't remember how to join them. Once, when I talked myself into going to a wedding reception, I only lasted for about ten minutes. I was in a crowd of people laughing and talking and celebrating, and it felt like Mars.

Hardly anybody knew how far I had slipped. Sometimes I was afraid that, if people saw what grief had done to me, they would want to get away from me. And I wouldn't have blamed them because most of the time I wanted to get away from me, too.

Even on the days when I wasn't trying to keep people out, I didn't have the hope or the energy or the words to invite them in. The grief felt too deep and too private to share. That's why, when people asked how I was doing, I kept saying *fine*. It was just easier that way.

Even though I usually couldn't let people in, knowing that they wanted to come in was a lifeline. When I was barely hanging on, it helped to remember the friend whose knock I couldn't answer—the one who left me a voicemail message later that day saying that she would do anything for me. I carried that offer around like some concentration camp survivors carried a slice of bread—just in case.

Even when I was desperate, I could usually carry on fairly well in the business arena. The grief didn't seem to touch that part of life. It only derailed my heart. The result was that I looked competent and in control, but on the inside I felt like a helpless child. One day I broke an hourglass that I loved, and I sat on my office floor in the middle of the mess and cried like a baby. It's not exactly the image you want to portray to the world at large. Luckily, I work from home.

Some days, just getting out of bed took all the energy I could muster. Things to do kept piling up and clamoring for my attention, but I had trouble getting started on any of them, and, worse, I had trouble caring. Time seemed to creep by. My thinking was fuzzy. Between the mental fog and the lethargy, even small things looked like mountains. I guess I was in good company because C. S. Lewis experienced the same sort of things after his wife died. He said, "It doesn't seem worth starting anything. I can't settle down. I yawn, I fidget, I smoke too much. Up till this, I always had too little time. Now there is nothing but time."[25]

Grief can have all sorts of strange physical manifestations, too. I found that my body had a whole grieving process of its own, and all I could do was watch. Even when my mind forgot about the grief for a while, my body remembered.

Sometimes it was a struggle just to take a deep breath. It felt like somebody was sitting on my chest. Sometimes, when I swallowed, it hurt from my throat to my stomach. On bad days, there was a constant low-grade nausea. Often I was lumbering and clumsy, as if the grief had sabotaged all my motor skills.

During the last years of my father's life, he had that ringing-in-the-ears syndrome called tinnitus. As soon as he died, like magic, I had it, too. On bad days, it seemed louder than everything else.

I had trouble sleeping, too. No matter how exhausted I was—and grief is exhausting—sleep was hard to come by. I would go to bed bone-weary and stare at the ceiling, and usually I would do the same thing all over again in the middle of the night.

There was no predicting when these symptoms would come and go. Sometimes they would disappear for a while and then, with no warning, they would ambush me again. Pascal said, "The heart has its reasons that reason knows not of."[26] And so, I found out, does the body. When your heart breaks, some things in your body break, too.

There were crazy emotional ups and downs. One day I would feel like life was good again, and the next day I could hardly face another minute. One day I would feel like joy was back for good, and the next day despair would be lapping at the shore again.

Sometimes whole weeks were black beyond all reckoning, and then, all of a sudden, a tender shoot of hope would spring up from the parched ground. But it wouldn't last. Just when things seemed to be getting better, I would find myself back in the same familiar dark hole. All I wanted was some consistent forward momentum, but most days felt like one step forward and at least two steps back. As C. S. Lewis described it:

> Tonight all the hells of young grief have opened again; the mad words, the bitter resentment, the fluttering in the stomach, the nightmare unreality, the wallowed-in tears. For in grief nothing "stays put." One keeps on emerging from a phase, but it always recurs. Round and round. Everything repeats. Am I going in circles, or dare I hope I am on a spiral?[27]

For a long time, the backward, dark days seemed to be winning. I kept getting more brokenhearted and more isolated. It reminded me of a game we used to play at the neighborhood pool when we were little. We would start in the shallow end and keep walking out into the deeper water until only our toes were touching the bottom and our mouths were just barely above the surface. Whoever went deepest won the game. That's what grief felt like, only I couldn't figure out how to stop playing, even when I could hardly breathe.

Most of the time, I was plagued by anxiety. Before Papa died, I didn't worry much at all, but afterward everything scared me. It was as if the grief of losing him unearthed all the smaller sadnesses and uncertainties and losses in my life. I lived with a vague, murky uneasiness. I would wake up in the middle of the night in the clutches of a cold and clammy dread. It was as if my subconscious knew that something was wrong even before I was awake enough to remember what it was. Then all the reasons to feel afraid would come pouring in.

The list was long, but the root fear, the one from which all the others seemed to sprout, was the fear that I would always feel alone and bereft and desperate and homeless. That fear lived with me. Sometimes it lived on the surface where I could see it, and sometimes it was hidden from view. Either way, it colored everything.

Tears were usually lurking just below the surface. I held them at bay as much as I could when other people were around, but they always caught up with me.

Life seemed drenched in pain (mine and everybody else's), and for the first time I started to lose my taste for it. I couldn't remember why my days used to sparkle with hope. The things I used to enjoy—being outside and sharing a good meal and talking with friends—all seemed flat and dull.

I hardly even recognized my own heart. Before Papa died, I had lived happily in the familiar parts of it, but afterward I found myself stumbling around in the dark, unexplored parts. It felt like all the old, comfortable rooms were locked up, closed for the season. I hardly knew myself. Who was this person who couldn't make a simple decision? Who was this person who couldn't wait for guests to go home? Who was this person who yelled at the dog just for being there?

My whole life felt like the day back in college when a burglar ransacked my apartment. Everything was upside down. Clothes were thrown everywhere. Things I loved were gone or broken. The place that had been home was ruined. I took what was left of my things and walked out the door and never went back. That's exactly what happened when Papa died. Everything was upside down and broken, but I couldn't get away from the mess. All I could do was wander around trying to remember what normal used to look like and wondering whether I would ever feel at home anywhere again.

In a way, it was like living in the Good Samaritan story.[28] There are four people in the story—the man lying beaten and half-dead on the road, the man who stops to help him, and the two men who cross the street to avoid him. Before Papa died, I saw myself as either the man who helped or one of the two who didn't. It never occurred to me that I could be the one lying on the road, wounded and helpless.

Who-am-I questions plagued me during the day and kept me awake at night. Sooner or later, they always led to *Who-is-God* questions—or, to be more honest, *Where-is-God* (and even *Is-there-a-God*) questions. It was terrifying and disorienting. I had lived most of my life on the rock-solid foundation of knowing that God was with me and for me, but sometimes, on the darkest days of grieving, I couldn't find Him. It felt like He had forgotten me, or, worse, like He was a figment of my imagination.

In all the disorientation, up started to feel like down to me. I've heard that happens to pilots in bad storms. They have to trust the instruments, because the storm makes it hard to tell which way is *up* and which way is *down*.

Grief is like that. You can't navigate through the storm by doing what *feels* right because what feels right could be the opposite of right.

This sounds strange because most of us live most of our lives making choices based on how we feel. When you're grieving, that system breaks down. You start to realize, maybe for the first time, that you need an instrument panel. You need something solid and stable to navigate by, because you can't rely on your feelings to tell you which way is up.

But what else is there? If you can't navigate on the basis of how you feel, what can you rely on? For me, it was the Scriptures. I followed them, even when they didn't feel true at all—even when, on the darkest days, they felt like lies.

Here's what I mean. In the worst of the grief, my feelings told me that God had completely forgotten me. It felt like He had left, and He wasn't ever coming back. It felt like I was on my own, and I would be lost and broken forever. Life felt precarious and capricious and terrifying. The feelings were so strong that they seemed like rock-solid truth, so it was hard work to cling to what Scripture says—that God will never forsake me[29] and that His love for me is as high as the heavens are above the earth.[30] I had to keep choosing, over and over again, to rest my weary weight on the words of Scripture instead of on my feelings. Sometimes it took every scrap of energy and perseverance I had. I read the Scriptures and wrote them down and said them out loud and even memorized them. I recited them over and over again in the middle of the night. I prayed them, and I cried them. They were my solid ground, especially when it came to dealing with all the fear that grief brought in its wake.

I had known for years that Scripture invites me to hand all my fears to God instead of trying to carry them myself,[31] but mostly I had managed them on my own anyway. After Papa died, there were so many fears that the weight was crushing me. So, over and over again, I handed God the fears. I handed Him the fears about having nothing to give to the people I loved. I handed Him the sickening, nagging questions about whether my life would ever amount to anything. I kept giving Him the burden of all the haunting thoughts about all the bad choices I had made over the years and all the chances I had missed—things that I had hardly ever thought about until grief somehow put them front-and-center. I had to be aggressive about not listening to the feelings that told me it was too late and life was hopeless and God didn't care anyway.

Please don't misunderstand me. I'm saying that it is dangerous to *follow* your feelings, but I'm not in any way suggesting that you bury them or be ashamed or afraid of them. That would make you sick. You have to bring your feelings out into the light and give them fresh air so they can heal. As Henri Nouwen said, "The great challenge is living your wounds through instead of thinking them through. It is…better to feel your wounds deeply than to understand them."[32] This is hard, especially in the midst of grief, when so many feelings seem dark and ugly and scary.

The Bible doesn't tiptoe around this. All the darkest feelings are right there in black and white. There are starkly honest words that were spoken by people who felt hopeless and forgotten and forsaken. There are dark words spoken by people who went far deeper into suffering than most of us will ever go.

I found that, when I had no words to express my grief, I could use words from Scripture. Jesus did. When He cried out from the cross, "My God, my God, why have You forsaken me?,"[33] He was speaking words from Scripture. When He was in the agony of forsakenness, Scripture words articulated His grief. They articulated mine, too.

Scripture also reminded me that, no matter how alone I might feel in my grief, I wasn't alone. I was on a well-worn path. Many people had walked it before me, and many people will walk it after me. My little world is just that—one small part of a much bigger picture. Gradually, in fits and starts, I began to see that I was part of a vast brotherhood. This truth helped me to look up, and it kept me out of the swamps of self-pity—at least on the good days. I needed that protection desperately when I was grieving because most of the time it felt like my dark and lonely world was the center of a dark and lonely universe.

Listen to these words:

> *I am faint. Heal me, O Lord, for my bones are in agony. My soul is in deep anguish…. How long, O Lord? Will you forget me forever? How long will you hide your face from me?…Will the Lord reject forever? Will He never show His favor again? Has His unfailing love vanished forever? Has His promise failed for all time? Has God forgotten to be merciful? Has He in anger withheld his compassion?*[34]

Do you hear the *forever* fear in these words from Scripture? There are so many *forevers* that any good editor would delete most of them, but they are there, over and over again, because that's how grief feels. It feels like forever. It feels like you'll never find solid ground again. It feels exactly like this:

> *[T]he waters have come up to my neck. I sink in the miry depths, where there is no*

foothold. I have come into the deep waters;
the floods engulf me. I am worn out calling
for help; my throat is parched. My eyes fail,
looking for my God.[35]

When you're grieving, these words and others like them can be a refuge and a relief. They spell out all the darkness and fear and exhaustion that you're so ashamed and afraid of, and they promise that, no matter how far you might go into this dark and painful tunnel, God has gone farther. In the words of Richard Baxter from centuries past, "Christ leads me through no darker rooms than He went through before."[36]

So it is safe to bring all your scary, tangled emotions into the light. You don't have to hide them because God knows them already. He has lived them. He has felt alone and bereft, too, and He has asked *Why have You forsaken me?* You can borrow His question. You can ask that same terrible question and feel the awful pain of the forsakenness without embarrassment or apology or shame.

That freedom is really important because it's easy to be ashamed of grief. I was. I was ashamed of having so little courage and so little faith (as I saw faith then), and I desperately needed the relief of seeing all my darkness and despair in the pages of the Bible. It gave me permission to feel all the dark feelings instead of trying to hide them or make them presentable. It showed me that tears could be a gift, relieving the pressure of the sadness and clearing the air like a good rain. It gave me the courage to be still enough to face the pain and feel it fully. That is crucial. Emotions never get healed if you keep them hidden.

I see grieving people hiding their feelings a lot, and it makes me sad. They say things like, "It's just silly. What I'm going through is nothing compared with what So-and-So is going through, and look at him. He's fine." I understand, because I did the same thing for a long time. I kept comparing myself to all the people around me who had lost huge parts of their lives and seemed to be getting "back to normal" a lot faster than I was. But this kind of thinking is poisonous. It forces your heart into hiding, and it keeps grief from being what it is meant to be—fruitful. That's right. Fruitful. Not productive, but fruitful.

If you're going to grieve well, you need to know the difference between productive and fruitful. "Productive" is just what it sounds like—producing and getting things accomplished and checking things off lists. It means making progress that you can see and measure and show to other people. Our culture values things that fall into the productive category. As long as you can produce, you get accolades. We all know this intuitively by the time we get to kindergarten, so most of us race around for most of our lives being productive and getting kudos for it.

"Fruitful" is something altogether different. Some of the most fruitful things you do—the things that bear good fruit in your life and in the lives of other people—seem like a waste of time in a culture that is fixated on productivity.

Here's what I mean. You can be fruitful while you're stuck in traffic—you can pray for somebody or sing a good song or enjoy the blue sky or be thankful that you're alive—but you can't be productive until the traffic clears. That's why productive people white-knuckle their way through traffic jams. They honk and pound the steering wheel because they can't get anything done while they're held up in traffic. And that's exactly what grief does—it holds you up like a giant traffic jam. It won't let you be the productive person you were before grief hit. That might sound like very bad news, but it isn't, because grief can change you from being productive to being fruitful.

In fact, the time of grieving may be the most fruitful season of your life. Grief can be fruitful, not because in the midst of it you roll up your sleeves and get busy doing things, but because, when you're flattened and you can't do anything at all, God creates. He creates in the darkness of the grief, when you don't think that anything good is happening in you (or that it ever will). God does remarkable things in the dark, when you least expect it. That's how He works. He was born in the middle of the night in a dark stable, and He rose in the middle of the night in a dark cave. That's how He grows plants, too. You'd never suspect that miracles could be happening under frozen ground and inside bare trees, would you? That's because you can't see how fruitful winter is until spring comes.

You see this in the Bible in the story of Naomi. She was living in a foreign country when her husband and her two sons died. She went back to her homeland bereft, alone except for one daughter-in-law. From Naomi's point of view, it looked like her family and her hope had been wiped out: "[T]he Almighty has made my life very bitter. I went away full, but the Lord has brought me back empty."[37] In the middle of the pain, she couldn't see the big picture. She couldn't see that her daughter-in-law would marry again and have a baby and that, generations later, from that baby would come a Baby born in a stable. She was in the winter of grief, and she thought spring had disappeared forever.

That's how it is with grief. Things get so dark that spring starts to seem like a pipe dream. But it isn't. Spring is coming. In the deep nether regions of your heart, God is re-creating. He is expanding the narrow, constricted places and making things new and spacious. Here's how C. S. Lewis describes it:

> *Imagine yourself as a living house. God comes in to rebuild that house. At first, perhaps, you can understand what He is doing. He is getting the drains right and stopping the leaks in the roof and so on; you knew that those jobs needed doing and so you are not surprised. But presently He starts knocking the house about in a way that hurts abominably and does not seem to make any sense. What on earth is He up to? The explanation is that He is building quite a different house from the one you thought of—throwing out a new wing here, putting on an extra floor there, running up towers, making courtyards. You thought you were being made into a decent little cottage: but He is building a palace. He intends to come and live in it Himself.*[38]

This is the big picture of grieving. You are God's work of art, and He is making you whole. He is freeing you from all the self-words that make you miserable and keep you isolated: self-enclosure, self-consciousness, self-pity, self-protectiveness, even self-reliance. He is healing your broken heart—not patching it up to get you "back to normal", but giving you a new and enlarged heart, whole and healthy and overflowing with joy. He is creating in you a heart that is free to love Him and to love other people, a heart that is content and peaceful, no matter what the circumstances. When He is finished, your heart will be a palace fit for a King. Once you see this big picture, you can say this prayer with St. Augustine, "My soul is like a house, small for you to enter, but I pray you to enlarge it. It is in ruins, but I ask you to remake it."[39]

People who haven't grieved yet usually don't think they need much re-creating. I didn't. I thought I was doing just fine. Sure, maybe there were a few things that I needed to work on, but basically I thought I was in pretty good shape. Apparently, that's not quite the way God sees it. In His eyes, we're wretched and pitiful and poor and blind and naked.[40] How's that for an addition to your resume? Sounds a little extreme, doesn't it? Well, yes…until you're in the throes of grief and your can-do, functional self shatters into a million pieces. That's when you start to take Him seriously when He says that, apart from Him, you can't do anything.[41] And that's when you start to get healthy because you stop relying on your own flimsy resources. You learn to say, like the prodigal son, "[H]ere I am starving to death! I will set out and and go back to my father…."[42]

When you do that, you find that your Father has

been waiting for you all along, even when it felt like He had deserted you. He is near the brokenhearted in a way that is too deep and mysterious for words.[43] He sees and feels all your brokenness, and it breaks His heart, too. He sees you with compassion, and He wants you to be free and whole.[44] That's why He is knocking and calling.

He always has been knocking and calling, but it's hard to listen when you think you have the world by the tail. In the pain and desperation of grief, you can learn to listen and you can choose, over and over again, to open the door of your heart to His invitation to grieve with you.

He does grieve with you.[45] You have never suffered alone, not even for one minute. None of your pain has gone unnoticed. As a friend reminded me, there is always a fourth Person in the fiery furnace. He was referring to the time when a king of old threw three men into a furnace to die. When the king looked into the furnace afterward, he saw the three men walking around unharmed, and with them was a Fourth.[46]

God is with you when you grieve, no matter how alone you feel. He is a sorrowing God, "a man of suffering, and familiar with pain."[47] In the words of William Blake, "[t]ill our grief is fled and gone, He doth sit by us and moan."[48] He is below you, around you, in you—His Spirit in your poor clay. *Parakletos*, the Greek word for the Holy Spirit, means the one who comes alongside to provide everything you could ever need.[49] In grief, you find out what you couldn't have known before—that you need everything.

Oddly, that is a relief. It means that you can relax and live the way you were created to live—walking humbly with your God, totally dependent on Him, sheltered by Him.[50] When Jesus wept over Jerusalem, He said, "[H]ow often I have longed to gather your children together, as a hen gathers her chicks under her wings, but you were not willing."[51] In the midst of grieving, you can run to Him and hide. You don't have to be ashamed of needing a hiding place. You don't have to be embarrassed about being a wreck. He sees you with compassion, so you can dare to see yourself with compassion, too. Instead of beating yourself up and lecturing yourself about what you should be doing and feeling, you can come to your Father and say, "Lord, the one You love is sick."[52] They are healing words, once you get used to them. After a while, you start to believe Him when He promises to turn your "valley of trouble" into a door of hope.[53]

If your life feels like a valley of trouble right now, take heart. God is true to His word. Keep choosing to turn toward Him and to rely on Him, and He will turn your interior desert into a garden. When the grief subsides, wonder of unexpected wonders, you'll find yourself in the midst of a new and inexplicable joy.[54] The grand surprise is that you will find in His friendship all the things you were frantically looking for before the grieving began. You find a hiding place. You find yourself loved. You find home.

In the end, you find that sorrow and joy are friends. You don't have to get rid of sorrow in order to know joy. Joy, it turns out, isn't some ephemeral thing that flits in and out of reach with the vagaries of mood and circumstance. It is solid and sure, and it is found in God's presence.[55] When you look for joy apart from Him, you won't find it—not because He hides it, but because real, solid, unshakeable joy lies only in friendship with Him. With infinite patience and kindness, through all the pain of grief, He woos you into that friendship.

This frees you to helicopter over the terrain of life, viewing its ups and downs from a higher vantage point. You might think that such a radical shift in perspective would detach you from the day-to-day, but it does just the opposite. This above-the-fray point of view frees you from the fear and self-protectiveness that keep you from fully engaging in the day-to-day. It frees you to enjoy the present moment. It opens to you the mysterious sacredness of the moment, so that you can live in contentment.

People who are content with God alone have a

quiet trust that He will give them everything that is good for them. They don't live in dread of bad news, and they don't compare and resent.

Barbara, through the ups and downs of multiple sclerosis, lives in that freedom. I remember the day I told her that I was going to Alaska. Her face lit up. She said, "How wonderful! Spencer and I have always wanted to go to Alaska." She hardly ever gets to leave her house, but she lives in the child-like confidence that, if her Father wanted her to go to Alaska, He certainly would send her there, so she doesn't envy my going. Hers is the freedom of a well-loved child. It is the freedom born of grieving well.

With this freedom to live fully and contentedly in the moment comes something else that is unexpected—a new and fresh expectation of heaven. Like so many things about grieving, this sounds upside down at first. If you're being freed to enjoy the moment, how can you at the same time be anticipating heaven? I can't answer that, except to share this one small hint: there is something about knowing present joy that whets your appetite and prepares you for the land of joy.

And that's what heaven is. The problem is that, when most people think about heaven, they don't think of overflowing joy. They think of being bored to death…forever. They think that our needs and desires are too big for heaven, but they have it backwards. The truth is that we're too small for heaven, and that's why God is re-creating us here. He is enlarging our souls, often through pain, in order to fit us for heaven:

> *For in every moment of our days, when once our hearts are yielded to His service, God is working in us.... Hitherto, perhaps, our little world has only been large enough to hold self and the present. But, gradually, through tender leadings and unfoldings, and, it may be, through pain and suffering, we come to learn life's lesson— that it is God's world, not ours; that our existence is not finished and rounded off here, but forms part of one vast scheme to which mind and heart and spirit expand and grow, while all the horizon round them grows and expands, too, until it touches the shore of the illimitable future, and we become conscious that earth and heaven are not so far separated, but that the first is but the vestibule of the second.*[56]

Heaven is more than our small selves can grasp. It is the fulfillment of all the desires of our hearts. It is the healing of all our brokenness. It is the end of all our fears. It is the love we've always wanted. The years we spend on earth aren't the main show.

They're just the dress rehearsal. The curtain hasn't even gone up yet. In the words of William Blake, "[W]e are put on earth a little space / that we may learn to bear the beams of love."[57]

There is no suffering in heaven. He will wipe every tear from your eyes. You won't hunger or thirst. There won't be any mourning or crying or pain. There won't be any death—and that doesn't just mean that people won't die. It means that dreams won't die and desires won't die and friendships won't die. Nothing good will die.[58]

People who have grieved well know that no price is too high to pay to fit us for the bliss that lies ahead. They can say with Archbishop Fenelon, "Tear away everything—down to the roots—everything that would take Your place within me…. All that I suffer is meant to find relief in You."[59] They can live grateful and contented lives, even in the midst of searing pain.

I'm not suggesting that you go looking for suffering or that you give thanks for bad things like disease and divorce and death. I'm saying that, in the midst of them, you can choose to give thanks no matter how you feel. You can thank God for being in complete control and for heaven and for walking with you in the fiery furnace and for orchestrating your circumstances for your ultimate good.[60] You can thank Him for guiding you through the murky darkness when you can't see anything at all. As Barbara said when the doctors couldn't figure out how to manage her pain, "I'm so thankful that this is as clear as crystal to the Divine Physician." She calls this kind of thinking "aggressive thanksgiving"— choosing to live over the circumstances instead of under them.

The author Joni Eareckson Tada is another person who has learned to live over her circumstances. She has been a quadriplegic since a diving accident decades ago, and she lives in the sure knowledge that her paralyzed arms and legs are merely things of earth. In heaven (if not sooner), she knows that she will run and dance. Like Barbara, she knows that God can take away her disability any time He wants to, and she trusts that, if that were best for her, He would.

Can you hear the freedom in this perspective— the openness to God and the absence of self-focus and self-pity? It is the fruit of years of choosing to grieve well. These two women have seen their souls enlarged as they have lived in child-like trust in their Father's love. Freed from the burden of looking out for Number One, they have discovered the joy of surrender. Their grief has been the gateway to loving God and themselves and other people.

Learning to grieve well isn't easy. It takes a long time, and you need people who will wait with you. You need friends. Even Jesus needed friends. In the end, just before He was arrested, He gathered His three closest friends and said, "My soul is overwhelmed with sorrow to the point of death."[61] He asked them to stay with Him, but they didn't have the courage. They fell asleep while He was in anguish, and then, after He was arrested, they ran away and deserted Him. I understand that now. Staying with somebody who is grieving is scary and undoing.

For one thing, it's hard to know what to say to someone who is grieving. People want to be comforting and encouraging, but sometimes their well-intentioned words sound a lot like *shoulds*.

Here's an example. After Papa died, a lot of people said things like, "You must be so thankful that your father had lived such a long and full life." This was hard for me to hear. On the one hand, of course, I *was* thankful, but, on the other hand, his living until eighty-nine made the loss bigger. I knew that people meant well, but it highlighted for me how careful you have to be when you're talking to someone who is in pain. It doesn't take much to send them into hiding. They're quick to hear *should,* which only adds guilt to the grief.

Should comments can be like knives to the heart. One couple I know lost their infant son, and within weeks people were reminding them to be thankful because God knew what He was doing when He took the child. I'm sure those people were only trying to ease the pain, but instead they multiplied it by adding guilt and confusion to the grief. They caused the grieving parents to lock up their hearts and bury their pain, forcing them deeper into isolation.

What you need desperately when you're in pain is someone who will listen without judging or labeling or fixing, because one of the few things you still want to do is talk about the loss—the person you lost or the health you lost or whatever it is that's breaking your heart.

Every time I visited my mother after Papa died, we talked about him. We talked about every detail of his last day—what he said, what he ate for dinner, whom Mom called after calling 911. Every time we talked about him, it eased the pain a little.

I was usually looking for chances to talk about him, but most people didn't know that, so they carefully avoided mentioning him. His death became the elephant in the room. I tried not to raise the subject too much either because I didn't want to make people even more uncomfortable around me than they already were.

With the people closest to me, I talked about him more, but even with them I was self-conscious about my conversations seeming like reruns. They had heard all the stories about him before, and I was pretty sure they were tired of them. The problem was that I wanted to keep telling those stories. The reruns felt good to me. It was like letting sunshine into a dark room. For reasons I still can't explain, I needed to have somebody see what I saw and feel what I felt. I needed the relief of not feeling alone, even if it was just for a few minutes. People who had suffered a lot understood this, so they could listen without feeling pressured to fix things or give advice. They knew there was no quick fix. They knew it would be a long road.

I'm not suggesting that there is no place for wise and healing words. There is. In fact, the healing words that friends spoke to me during my grief were treasures. I thought about them over and over again. I still think about them.

On one particularly dark day, I called a friend and told him how lost and empty I was and how terrible I felt about having nothing to offer. He said, "Of course, you have nothing to give right now, my dear. You are wounded, and you must be gentle with yourself." I can still feel the relief of those kind words. They were the opposite of *shoulds*. He wasn't telling me to shape up and try harder to get back to normal. He was saying that I needed to give myself a break. He was giving me permission to stop pushing. He was encouraging me to give my heart a little compassionate space. When I told him that I was thinking of going back to full-time law practice (which I hadn't done in years), he said, "Well, that may be a good idea, but remember that it will only be a Band-Aid." As soon as I heard his words, I knew he was right. The full-time lawyering idea was just my way of trying to shore up my functional identity so that I could hide behind it and keep the pain at bay. He saw what I couldn't see, and he helped me stay on track.

You need that when you're in the fog of grief. One day I told a friend that I had decided not to write anymore because my world had gotten so dark that everything I wrote was dark, too. She listened for a long time, and she watched me with kind eyes. Then she told me to keep writing. She said, "It won't always be this dark, and the things that God shows you in the dark will encourage other people coming along behind you." At that point, I couldn't imagine ever being any help to anybody, but I trusted her, so I kept writing. She told me that, in God's economy, nothing is wasted. She said that He would use my grief for His good purposes. That seemed impossible, too, but she was right.

She could see what I couldn't see—that, even though my dark days weren't productive, they were fruitful. She called it a time of pruning, and she said that the pruning was a kindness. She told me that, through the pain, God would enlarge my heart and teach me to trust Him more and give me deeper compassion for other people. "Revel in the darkness," she said. "You have to learn to revel in the darkness."

She told me these things with shining eyes, because she had lived them. She was far ahead of me on the path of grieving, and her life was full of hope. In those dark days when I had no hope, she offered me hers.

My children did, too. Being on empty and having nothing to offer was hardest with them. For over twenty years, I had showered them with time and attention and love. I had comforted them when they were hurt and encouraged them when they were down. Then Papa died, and in the blink of an eye the roles were reversed. They loved me when I had nothing to give in return. They listened gently, and they hugged me, and they cried with me. They talked about Papa with me. I tried to hide the worst of the grief from them because I didn't want to scare them and I didn't want to be a burden to them, but it didn't work. They could see right through me. Now I'm glad that I couldn't hide from them, because the role reversal was good for all of us. It made us closer friends. Before Papa died, I didn't think it was possible to love my children more. I was wrong.

The same sort of thing happened in my marriage. No matter how far I slid, my husband never budged. He was rock solid. He held me when I cried. Month after month, he picked his way bravely through the land mines of all my fearful *what if* questions. He listened. He let me talk about the loss and the pain and the memories without having to compete for airtime and without worrying about how many times I had said it all before. At the beginning, I was afraid that the grief would separate us, but it didn't. It did the opposite. It made us more vulnerable and more honest and, in the end, more light-hearted. It led us deeper into friendship.

There were also unlikely friends. One night, not long after Papa died, I went to a church service for people who needed healing. I knelt at the altar rail, and two older ladies prayed for me in their soft Southern accents. "Lawd, we thank ya for Carlton's life." They said thank you for the gift of a father who loved so well. They said thank you because all his pain was gone and because one day he and I would be together again. For a long time afterward, I sat in my pew, basking in hope. They were friends for a night, easers of pain, reminders of truth.

Some authors were friends, too. Jerry Sittser was one. In *A Grace Disguised,* he talks about losing his wife and his mother and his daughter in a head-on collision with a drunk driver. For a long time after the accident, he lost heart, and he thought he had lost his faith. In a strange way, it was a relief to me to hear him say that. He had asked the same

Where-is-God questions that I was asking. He had gone through the same dark tunnel, and he had come out into the light again. He had seen grief start to bear fruit in his life. Years after the accident, he said that he had a new sense of the sacredness of the present moment:

> *Never have I felt as much pain...yet never have I experienced as much pleasure in simply being alive.... Never have I felt so broken; yet never have I been so whole. Never have I been so aware of my weakness and vulnerability; yet never have I been so content and felt so strong.... What I once considered mutually exclusive—sorrow and joy, pain and pleasure, death and life—have become parts of a greater whole. My soul has been stretched.*[62]

People who have grieved well, keeping their hearts open to God in the midst of their pain, can offer hope because they have already walked the canyon floor. They know how it feels. They know the pain, and they know God's comfort. They are, as Henri Nouwen puts it, "wounded healers"—healers, not because they are strong, but because they have discovered their own weakness and God's strength. [63]

That's how things work in the world of grief. The

wounded, if they are good stewards of their pain, become healers. They get comfortable with being "wretched, pitiful, poor, blind and naked,"[64] so they stop spinning and dancing. They stop trying to hold together a fragile functional identity. They know that we were never meant to have an identity apart from God and apart from each other. They have become persons—loved by God and loving other people. They are the ones you seek out when you hurt, even if you've never heard their story. You can see it in their eyes. You can sense it in their presence. They are friends, even if you hardly know them.

> *Are there not some in your circle to whom you naturally betake yourself in times of trial and sorrow? They always seem to speak the right word, to give the very counsel you are longing for. You do not realize, however, the cost which they had to pay ere they became so skillful in binding up the gaping wounds and drying tears. But if you were to investigate their past history you would find that they have suffered more than most. They have watched the slow untwisting of some silver cord on which the lamp of life hung. They have seen the golden bowl of joy dashed to their feet, and its contents spilt. They have stood by ebbing tides and drooping gourds and*

noon sunsets, but all this has been necessary to make them the nurses, the physicians, the priests of men.... So suffering is rough and hard to bear, but it hides beneath it discipline, education, possibilities, which not only leave us nobler, but perfect us to help others. Do not fret or set your teeth or wait doggedly for the suffering to pass, but get out of it all you can, both for yourself and for your service to your generation.[65]

Grief can be a gateway to new life if you let it enlarge your heart. It isn't easy. It takes courage. The old you isn't big enough to grieve deeply, so you'll grow and change a lot. You'll never get back to the "normal" you knew before, but you won't want to. Who would trade the constant effort of trying to make something of yourself for the relief of God making something of you? Who would cling to the old functional identity once you start to see who you really are (and who God really is)?

In the midst of my grief, I was afraid that, when the floodwaters subsided, I would find myself a stranger in a strange land, unable to do the things I used to do, to enjoy the things I used to enjoy, to love the people I used to love. But it wasn't true. I *am* different now, but not in the way I had feared. I feel more substantial. I love the people around me more (maybe because I need them less). There is more compassion and less self-focus. There is more joy—a solid sort of joy that is deeper than the ups and downs of circumstances. Somehow tears and laughter have learned to live comfortably side-by-side.

Grief forced me to ask the hardest questions: *Is God there?* and *Is He good?* and *Is He good to me?* Now I know the answers—not just in my head, but also in my heart. I know Him now, with every fiber of my being, as the God who loves me. There is no greater gift.

Against all odds, grief is a love word.

It is a tremendous moment when first one is called upon to join the great army of those who suffer. That vast world of love and pain opens suddenly to admit us one by one within its fortress. We are afraid to enter into the land, yet you will, I know, feel how high is the call. It is as a trumpet speaking to us that cries aloud, "It is your turn—endure." Play your part. As they endured before you, so now, close up the ranks—be patient and strong as they were. Since Christ, this world of pain is no accident untoward or sinister, but a lawful department of life, with experiences, interests, adventures, hopes, delights, secrets of its own. These are all thrown open to us as we pass within the gates—things that we could never learn or know or see, so long as we were well. God help you to walk through this world now opened to you, as through a kingdom, royal and wide and glorious.[66]

"Those who sow in tears will reap with songs of joy. Those who go out weeping, carrying seed to sow, will return with songs of joy, carrying sheaves with them."

Psalm 126:5-6

Endnotes

1   Robert Frost and Edward Connery Lathem, "Lodged" In
    The Poetry of Robert Frost (New York: Holt, Rinehart and
    Winston, 1969), 250.

2   C. S. Lewis, *The Four Loves* (New York: Harcourt, Brace,
    1960), 96.

3   Dwight L. Moody, *The Overcoming Life* edited by Gene
    Fedele (Alachua, Fla.: Bridge-Logos, 2007), i.

4   Charles E. Cowman, "July 15" In *Streams in the Desert: 366
    Daily Devotional Readings* (Grand Rapids, Mich.: Zondervan
    Pub. House, 1997), 274.

5   "(676): To Theo van Gogh. Arles, Saturday, 8 September
    1888," In *Vincent van Gogh—The Letters, Van Gogh Museum*,
    (Amsterdam: Huygens ING, The Hague, 2009), http://
    vangoghletters.org/vg/letters/let676/letter.html.

Endnotes

6   Dinah Maria Craik, *A Life for a Life* (New York: Harper & Brothers, 1872), 169.

7   John Baillie. *A Diary of Private Prayer* (New York: Charles Scribner's Sons, 1949), 85.

8   Roger Lundin, *Emily Dickinson and the Art of Belief* (Grand Rapids, Mich.: William B. Eerdmans Pub., 1998), 177.

9   George Matheson, "O Love That Wilt Not Let Me Go" (1882) In *The United Methodist Hymnal: Book of United Methodist Worship* (Nashville, Tenn.: United Methodist House, 1989), 480.

10   Ann Voskamp, *One Thousand Gifts: A Dare to Live Fully Right Where You Are* (Grand Rapids, Mich.: Zondervan, 2010), 156.

11   William Blake and Sir Geoffrey Keynes, "On Another's Sorrow" In *Songs of Innocence and of Experience: Shewing the Two Contrary States of the Human Soul* (New York, Paris: The Orion Press in association with The Trianon Press, 1967), 27.

12   George MacDonald, *Unspoken Sermons* (New York: Cosimo, 2007), 205.

13   Anne Lamott, "Homage to Age and Femininity" In *O Magazine*.

14   "George Herbert: The Flower (1633)" In *The Metaphysical Poets* edited by Helen Gardner, 2nd ed. (Baltimore, Maryland: Penguin Books, 1968), 136.

15   George MacDonald, *The Diary of an Old Soul* (Minneapolis, Minn.: Filiquarian, 2007), 10.

16   Henri J. M. Nouwen, *The Inner Voice of Love: A Journey through Anguish to Freedom* (New York: Doubleday, 1996), 109-110.

17   "George Herbert: Easter (1633)" In *George Herbert and the Seventeenth-Century Religious Poets* edited by Mario A. Di Cesare (New York: W. W. Norton & Company, 1978), 18.

18   Wendell Berry, *Jayber Crow: A Novel* (Washington, D.C.: Counterpoint, 2000), 149-150.

19   Henry E. Manning, quoted by Mary W. Tileston, "November 5" In *Joy and Strength* (New York: Grosset and Dunlap, 1978), 310.

20   MacDonald, Diary of an Old Soul, 32.

21   Blaise Pascal and A.J. Krailsheimer, *Pensees* (London: Penguin, 1966), 423.

Endnotes

22 "I have told you these things, so that in Me you may have peace. In this world you will have trouble." John 16:33a

23 "I stand at the door and knock. If anyone hears My voice and opens the door, I will come in...." Revelation 3:20

24 Michael Casey, *Toward God: The Ancient Wisdom of Western Prayer* (Liguori, MO: Triumph Books, 1996), 6.

25 C. S. Lewis, *A Grief Observed* (New York: Bantam Books, 1980), 38-39.

26 Pascal, Blaise, and A.J. Krailsheimer. *Pensees* (London: Penguin, 1966), 423.

27 Lewis, *A Grief Observed*, 66-67.

28 "Jesus said, 'A man was going down from Jerusalem to Jericho, when he was attacked by robbers. They stripped him of his clothes, beat him and went away, leaving him half dead. A priest happened to be going down the same road, and when he saw the man, passed by on the other side. So too, a Levite, when he came to the place and saw him, passed by on the other side. But a Samaritan, as he traveled, came where the man was; and when he saw him, he took pity on him. He went to him and bandaged his wounds...." Luke 10:30-34

29   "[Christ] has said, 'Never will I leave you; never will I forsake you.'" Hebrews 13:5

30   "For as high as the heavens are above the earth, so great is His love for those who revere Him." Psalm 103:11

31   "Cast all your anxiety on Him because He cares for you." I Peter 5:7

32   Nouwen, *Inner Voice of Love*, 109.

33   "My God, my God, why have You forsaken me? Why are You so far from saving me, so far from my cries of anguish?" Psalm 22:1; "About three in the afternoon Jesus cried out in a loud voice, "Eli, Eli, lema sabachthani?" (which means "My God, my God, why have You forsaken me?")." Matthew 27:46

34   Psalm 6:2-3; Psalm 13:1; Psalm 77:7-9

35   Psalm 69:1-3

36   Richard Baxter, "Christ Leads Me Through No Darker Rooms" (1681) In *Hymnal: According to the Use of the Protestant Episcopal Church of the United States of America* (Philadelphia, Penn.: Claxton, Remsen & Haffelfinger, 1871), 486.

Endnotes

37   Ruth 1:20-21a

38   C. S. Lewis, *Mere Christianity: Comprising The Case for Christianity, Christian Behaviour, and Beyond Personality* (New York: Touchstone, 1996), 176.

39   R.S. Pine-Coffin, *The Confessions of Saint Augustine* (New York: Penguin Books, 1983), 24.

40   "You say, 'I am rich...and do not need a thing. But you do not realize that you are wretched, pitiful, poor, blind and naked." Revelation 3:17

41   "I am the vine; you are the branches.... Apart from Me you can do nothing." John 15:5

42   Luke 15:17-18

43   "The Lord is close to the brokenhearted and saves those who are crushed in spirit." Psalm 34:18

44   "He has sent Me to bind up the brokenhearted, to proclaim freedom for the captives and release from darkness for the prisoners...." Isaiah 61:1

45   "In all their distress He too was distressed...." Isaiah 63:9; "For You saw my affliction and knew the anguish of my soul." Psalm 31:7

46   "Then King Nebuchadnezzar leaped to his feet in amazement and asked his advisers, 'Weren't there three men that we tied up and threw into the fire?... I see four men walking around in the fire, unbound and unharmed, and the fourth looks like a son of the gods." Daniel 3:24-25

47   "He was despised and rejected by mankind, a man of suffering and familiar with pain." Isaiah 53:3

48   Blake, "Another's Sorrow," 27.

49   "I will ask the Father, and He will give you another Helper and Comforter, that He may be with you forever." John 14:16

50   "Come to Me, all you who are weary and burdened, and I will give you rest." Matthew 11:28; "The Lord is my shepherd.... He refreshes my soul." Psalm 23:1-2

51   Luke 13:34

52   "So the sisters sent word to Jesus, "Lord, the one you love is sick." John 11:3

53   "There I will give her back her vineyards, and I will make the Valley of Achor a door of hope." Hosea 2:15a

Endnotes

54   "The Lord will surely comfort Zion and will look with compassion on all her ruins; He will make her deserts like Eden, her wastelands like the garden of the Lord. Joy and gladness will be found in her, thanksgiving and the sound of singing." Isaiah 51:3

55   "You make known to me the path of life; You will fill me with joy in Your presence, with eternal pleasures at Your right hand." Psalm 16:11

56   Hetty Bowman, *Thoughts on the Christian Life; Or, Leaves from Letters* (London: William Hunt, 1872), 10.

57   Blake, "The Little Black Boy," 9-10.

58   "Gladness and joy will overtake them, and sorrow and sighing will flee away." Isaiah 35:10; "What is mortal will be swallowed up by life." 2 Corinthians 5:4; "He will wipe away every tear from their eyes. There will be no more death or mourning or crying or pain...." Revelation 21:4

59   Francois Fenelon and Robert J. Edmonson, *The Complete Fenelon* (Brewster, Mass.: Paraclete Press, 2008), 218.

60   "And we know that in all things God works for the good of those who love Him...." Romans 8:28

61   Mark 14:34

62   Gerald Lawson Sittser, *A Grace Disguised: How the Soul Grows through Loss* (Grand Rapids, Mich.: Zondervan Pub. House, 1996), 199.

63   Henri J. M. Nouwen, *The Wounded Healer: Ministry in Contemporary Society* (New York: Doubleday Image, 1979).

64   "You say, 'I am rich...and do not need a thing. But you do not realize that you are wretched, pitiful, poor, blind and naked." Revelation 3:17

65   Cowman, "December 10" In *Streams in the Desert*, 274.

66   Henry Scott Holland, quoted by Mary W. Tileston, "September 22" In *Joy and Strength* (New York: Grosset and Dunlap, 1978), 266.